WORDS OF
WARN
ING

FOR THOSE WAVERING BETWEEN
BELIEF AND UNBELIEF

CHARLES H. SPURGEON

ANEKO
PRESS

We love hearing from our readers. Please contact us at www.anekopress.com/questions-comments with any questions, comments, or suggestions.

Aneko Press

www.anekopress.com

Aneko Press, Life Sentence Publishing, and our logos are trademarks of
Life Sentence Publishing, Inc.
203 E. Birch Street
P.O. Box 652
Abbotsford, WI 54405

RELIGION / Faith

Paperback ISBN: 978-1-62245-500-3
eBook ISBN: 978-1-62245-501-0

10 9 8 7 6 5 4

Available where books are sold

Contents

Chapter 1

The Great World Prison and the Liberator

When I was preaching in Dover, England, the mayor of the town let us rent the old town hall for our service. As I was walking by the building, I noticed a large number of windows on the lower level with metal bars on them. These windows belonged to the prison cells where the prisoners were confined. It struck me as an unusual combination, that we would be preaching the gospel of liberty on one level of the building while there were prisoners of the law beneath us.

Perhaps the prisoners heard us when we sang praises to God, but the words of freedom above did not give them liberty, nor did the words of the song free them from their bonds. What an accurate picture this is of many people. We preach liberty to captives and proclaim the acceptable year of the Lord, but how many remain year after year in the bondage of Satan, slaves to sin? We send up our songs of praise joyously to our Father who is in heaven, but our praises cannot give them joy because their hearts are not used to gratitude. Some are mourning because of unpardoned sin. Others are weeping because of their ruined hopes, because they have looked for comfort where it can never be found.

This little circumstance fixed itself in my mind and impressed itself upon me in my private meditations. I daydreamed that some angelic warden was leading me along the corridors of this great world prison. He asked me to look into the various cells where the prisoners were confined, and he kept reminding me, as I looked sorrowful, that it is God who sets the prisoners free. *He who does justice unto the oppressed; who gives bread to the hungry. The LORD looses the prisoners* (Psalm 146:7).

The first cell is called the common prison – the ward of sin. All people have been prisoners here. Those who today live in perfect liberty once wore the heavy chains and were confined within the dark walls. I entered the cell, and instead of hearing cries of mourning and lament, I heard loud and repeated bursts of laughter. The atmosphere was boisterous and noisy. The profane were cursing and blaspheming. Others shouted as though they had found a great treasure.

I looked into the faces of some of the criminals and saw much happiness. Their attitude was that of wedding guests rather than prisoners. Walking back and forth, I noticed prisoners who boasted that they were free. When I spoke to them of their prison and urged them to escape, they resented my advice, saying, "We were born free and were never in bondage to anyone." *They answered him, We are Abraham's seed, and we have never served anyone; how sayest thou, Ye shall be set free?* (John 8:33).

They asked me to prove my words. When I pointed to the iron chains on their wrists, they laughed at me and said that the chains were ornaments that produced music as they moved. They said it was only my dull and depressing mind that made me talk of jangling shackles and jingling chains. There were men shackled hard and fast to foul and evil sins, and they called themselves free-livers, while others whose very thoughts were bound, because the iron had entered into their soul, cried out to me with proud looks that they were freethinkers.

I had never seen such prisoners before, nor any so securely bound as these. But one thing I noticed as I walked throughout this prison was that those most bound by chains and shackles thought themselves to be the most free, and those who were in the darkest part of the dungeon thought they had the most light. Those whom I considered to be the most wretched and the most to be pitied were the very ones who laughed the most and shouted most insanely and boisterously in their amusement.

I looked with sorrow, but then I saw a bright spirit touch a prisoner on the shoulder, who then withdrew with the shining one. He went out, and I knew that the prisoner had been loosed from the house of bondage, because I had read: *The LORD looses the prisoners.* As he departed, though, his fellow prisoners laughed, pointed their fingers, and called him hypocrite, pretender, and all sorts of cruel names, until the prison walls rang and rang again with their merry contempt. I watched and saw the mysterious visitor touch another, and another, and then another, and they disappeared.

The common conversation in the prison was that they had gone crazy or that they had become slaves or miserable fanatics. But I knew that they had gone to be free forever, set free from every bond. What struck me most was that the prisoners who were touched with the finger of delivering love were often the worst of the whole crew. I saw one who had blasphemed, but the divine hand touched him, and he went weeping out of the gate. I saw another who had often ridiculed the loudest when he had seen others led away, but he went out as quietly as a lamb. I observed some whom I thought to be the least depraved of them all, but they were left behind, while many times the worst sinners of the whole group were taken first. Then I remembered that I had read these words: *The publicans and the harlots go ahead of you into the kingdom of God* (Matthew 21:31).

As I looked intently, I saw some of those men who had once been prisoners come back again into the prison, not in the same clothing which they had worn before, but clothed in white robes, looking like new creatures. They spoke with their fellow prisoners, and oh, how sweetly they spoke! They told them there was liberty available to them, that the door would open, and that they could go free. They pleaded with their fellow men, even to the point of tears. I saw them sit down and talk with them until they wept upon their necks, urging them to escape, pleading as though it were their own life at stake.

At first, I hoped that the whole group of prisoners would rise and cry out, "Let us be free." But no; the more these men pleaded, the harder the hearts of the others seemed to become. That is also how I found it when I myself attempted to be an ambassador to these slaves of sin.

I asked the guide where those were taken who were released from the common ward. He told me that they were taken away to be free – completely free – but before they were allowed to be released, it was necessary for them to visit a certain place of detention. He led me toward that place. It was called the *solitary cell*. I had heard a lot about the solitary system, and I desired to look inside that cell, supposing it would be a dreadful place. Over the door was written this word: *Penitence*.

When I opened the door, I found the room so clean, white, sweet, and full of light, that I thought the place was more fit to be a house of prayer than a prison. My guide told me that it was indeed originally intended to be so, and that nothing but that iron door of unbelief that the prisoners persisted in shutting securely made it a prison at all. Once that door was open, the place became a precious, small chapel, so those who were once prisoners within wanted to come back to the cell of their own accord. They begged to use it, not as a prison, but as a room for prayer for the rest of their lives. He even told me that one man who was dying said that his only regret in dying was that in heaven there would be no cell of remorse and sorrow. Here, David wrote seven of his sweetest Psalms, Peter wept bitterly, and the woman who was a sinner washed the feet of her Lord.

But this time, I was regarding it as a prison, and I perceived that the person in the cell also considered it a prison. I learned that every prisoner in this cell must be there alone. He had grown accustomed to mix with the crowd and to find comfort in the belief that he was a Christian because he had been born in a Christian nation; but he learned that he must be saved alone if he was to be saved at all. He had been used to going up to the house of God with others, and he thought that simply going there was enough. But now, every sermon seemed to be aimed at him, and every admonition stung his conscience. I remember to have read in the ancient book of the prophet Zechariah:

> *And I will pour upon the house of David*
> *and upon the inhabitants of Jerusalem the*
> *Spirit of grace and of prayer, and they shall*
> *look upon me whom they have pierced, and*
> *they shall mourn over him as one mourns*
> *for his only son, afflicting themselves over*
> *him as one afflicts himself over his first-*
> *born. In that day there shall be a great*
> *mourning in Jerusalem as the mourning of*
> *Hadadrimmon in the valley of Megiddon.*
> *And the land shall mourn, each family*
> *apart; the family of the house of David*

> *apart, and their wives apart; the family of*
> *the house of Nathan apart, and their wives*
> *apart.* (Zechariah 12:10-12)

I noticed that the repentant one, while alone and apart in his cell, often sighed and groaned, and now and then, mingled with his penitent utterances, came some words of unbelief. Truly, if it were not for these, that heavy door would have been removed from its hinges long ago. It was unbelief that shut the prisoners in, and if unbelief had been removed from this cell, it would have been an oratory for heaven instead of a place for downhearted mourning and lamentation.

As the prisoner wept for his past, he prophesied for the future and groaned that he could never come out of this confinement, because sin had utterly ruined him and destroyed his soul eternally. It was clear that his fears were foolish, because as I looked around this clean, white cell, I saw that the door had a knocker inside, and that if the man had the courage to lift it, there was a shining one standing ready outside who would open the door at once. Yes, and even more, I perceived that there was a secret spring called *faith,* and if the man would just touch it, even though his finger might be trembling, it would make the door fly open.

Then I noticed that this door had the marks of blood on the top post and on the two side posts. Any man who looked on that blood, lifted that knocker, or touched that spring found the door of unbelief fly open, and he came out of the cell of his solitary remorse to rejoice in the Lord who had wiped away his sin and cleansed him forever from all iniquity.

I spoke to this remorseful prisoner and asked him to trust in the blood. It may be that through my words, the Lord afterward set the prisoner free. I learned, though, that no words of mine alone could do it, because in this case, even where repentance was mingled with just a little unbelief, it is the Lord, and the Lord alone, who can set the prisoner free.

I passed that cell and stopped at another. This one also had an iron gate of unbelief, as heavy and as huge as the one before. I heard the warden coming. When he opened the door for me, it creaked horribly on its hinges and disturbed the silence. This time, I had come into the *silent cell*. The reprobate confined here was one who said he could not pray. If he could pray, he would be free. He was groaning, crying, sighing, and weeping because he could not pray. All he could tell me, as he rolled his eyes in agony, was this: "I want to, but I cannot pray. I want to plead with God, but I cannot find any words, because my guilt has made me mute." Back he went and refused to speak again, but he kept up his desolate groaning all day long.

In this place, no sound was heard except that of wailing. All was quiet except the dropping of his tears upon the cold stone, and his dreary cries for mercy in sighs and groans. There was a little table in this cell on which lay a key of promise. The key was inscribed with these fine words: *For he has looked down from the height of his sanctuary; from the heavens the LORD beheld the earth to hear the groaning of the prisoner; to loose those that are appointed to death* (Psalm 102:19-20).

I thought that if this man cannot speak, God can still hear his groans. If he cannot plead, God listens to his sighs and sees him all the way from heaven, catching even the faintest whisper of this poor man's broken heart so that He might set him free. Even if the soul feels it can neither plead nor pray, it has still prayed, and it will prevail. I tried to catch the ear of my poor friend and talk to him for a little while, even though he would not speak. I reminded him that the Book in his cell contained instances of mute men whom Jesus had enabled to speak, and I told him that Christ was able to make him speak plainly, too.

I told the man that whether he could pray or not, he was commanded to look at the blood marks over his door. I reminded him that the publican was justified by the blood, even though he could only cry, *God, reconcile me, a sinner* (Luke 18:13). I pleaded with him to receive the Lord's own testimony, that the Lord Jesus is *able also to save to the uttermost those that come unto God by him* (Hebrews 7:25), that He was waiting to be gracious and was a God ready to pardon (Nehemiah 9:17). After all this, though, I felt that the Lord alone must set His prisoners free. Oh, gracious God, set them free now!

We moved quickly to a fourth door. The door opened and shut behind me as I stood alone. It was as dark as Egypt during the plague of darkness (Exodus 10:21-23)! This was the black hole called the *cell of ignorance.* I groped as a blind man gropes for the wall. The sounds of sobs and moans guided me to a spot where a man knelt in an earnest agony of prayer. I asked him what made his cell so dark. I knew the door was made of unbelief, which certainly shut out all light, but I wondered why this place was darker than the rest. Then I remembered reading about some who *sat in darkness and in the shadow of death, being bound in affliction and in irons* (Psalm 107:10).

I asked him if there were any windows in the cell. He said that he was told that there were many windows, but they had been sealed up years ago and he did not know how to open them. He was fully convinced that they could never provide him with light. I felt around for one of the old windows, but it seemed as if instead of giving light, it emitted darkness. I touched it with my hand, and it felt to me like it was a window just like others that had once given light and like those I have often looked through with delight.

He told me it was one of the doctrines of grace, called *election*, that had greatly perplexed him. The little light that fell upon the poor man led him to seek for more. Another darkened window was called *human depravity*. The man said, "Oh, there is no hope for me, because I am totally depraved. My nature is detestable and vile. There is no hope for me."

I pulled the rags from this window and said to him, "Do you not see that your ruin prepares you for the remedy? It is because you are lost that Christ came to save you. Physicians are for the sick, robes for the naked, cleansing for the filthy, and forgiveness for the guilty."

He said very little, but pointed to another window.

It was one I had looked through for a long time and through which I had seen my Master's glory. This was the doctrine of *particular redemption*.

"Ah!" he said. "Suppose Christ has not redeemed me with His precious blood! Suppose He never bought me with His death!"

I knocked out some old bricks that had been put in by an unskilled hand, yet still blocked out the light, and I told the man that Christ did not offer a counterfeit redemption, but one that really did redeem, because *the blood of Jesus Christ, his Son cleanses us from all sin* (1 John 1:7).

I continued on and came to another chamber. This room, marked number five, was large and had many people in it who were trying to walk back and forth. Every man had a chain around his ankle and a huge cannonball attached to it – a military punishment, they said, for deserters from the ranks of virtue. This encumbrance troubled the prisoners very much. I saw some of them trying to file their chains with rusty nails. Others endeavored to melt away the iron by dropping tears of remorse on it, but these poor men made little progress at their work. The warden told me that this was the chain of habit, and the ball that dragged behind was the old propensity to lust and sin.

> The proper way to get rid of the chain of habit was, first of all, to get out of prison.

I asked him why they had not been able to get their chains knocked off. He said they had been trying a long time to get rid of them, but they could never do it the way they were trying, since the proper way to get rid of the chain of habit was, first of all, to get out of prison. The door of unbelief must be opened, and they must trust in the one great Deliverer, the Lord Jesus, whose pierced hands could open all prison doors. After that, their bonds could be broken off upon the anvil of grace, with the hammer of love.

I saw a drunkard led out of his prison, rejoicing in pardoning grace. Prior to that time, he had tried to escape from his drunkenness, but three or four times he had broken his pledge and had gone back to his old sin. I saw that man trust in the precious blood, and he became a Christian. Once he became a Christian, he no longer loved to drink. With one stroke of the hammer, the ball was gone forever. Another man was a swearer who often took God's name in vain. He knew it was wrong to blaspheme the Most High, but he continued to do so until he gave his heart to Christ; then he never blasphemed again, because he hated that sin.

In almost all prisons where they do not want to make prisoners worse than when they entered, they have hard labor for them. In the prison I went to see, there was a *hard-labor room*. Those who entered it were mostly very proud people. They held their heads very high and would not bend. They were birds with fine feathers and thought themselves quite unfit to be confined, but being in dreadful captivity, they resolved to work their own way out. They believed in the system of human merit, and they hoped in due time to earn their freedom. They had saved up a few old counterfeit coins with which they thought they could set themselves free.

However, my bright attendant plainly declared their foolishness and mistake. It was amusing, yet sad, to see what different works these people were doing. Some of them toiled at the treadwheel. They said they were climbing to the stars, but there they were, treading with all their might; and even though they had been laboring for years and were not even an inch higher, they were still confident that they were climbing to the skies.

Others tried to make garments out of cobwebs. They turned wheels and spun at a great rate, and even though it came to nothing, they worked on. They believed they would be free as soon as they had made a perfect garment, and I believe they will.

In one place, a group of men labored to build houses of sand. When they had built up to some height, the foundations always failed, but they just started over. They dreamed that if they could build a large building, they would be allowed to go free. I saw some of them, strangely enough, attempting to make wedding garments out of fig leaves by sewing them together, but the fig leaves were of a type that shriveled every night, so that they had to start their hopeless toil all over again the next morning. Some, I noticed, were trying to pump water out of a dry well. The veins stood out upon their brows like whipcords while they worked with all their might, yet without result. As they labored like Samson when he was grinding at the mill, I could hear the crack of whips upon their backs.

I saw a ten-corded whip called the *Law* – the terrible Law – each cord being a commandment. This was laid upon the bare backs and consciences of the prisoners, yet they kept on working and would not turn to the door of grace to find escape. I saw some of them fall down fainting, and then their friends would try to bring them water in leaking vessels, called ceremonies. There were some men called priests, who ran around with cups that had no bottoms in them. They held these cups up to the lips of these poor fainting miserable men to attempt to give them comfort. As these men fainted, I thought they would die, but they struggled up again to work. At last they could do no more, and they fell down under their burdens, utterly broken in spirit. Then I saw that every prisoner who finally gave up all hope of his own deliverance by merit was taken up by a shining spirit and was carried out of the prison and made free forever.

I thought that these were certainly proud, self-righteous people who would not submit to being saved by grace. *Therefore he brought down their heart with labour; they fell down, and there was no one to help. Then they cried unto the LORD in their trouble, and he saved them out of their distresses* (Psalm 107:12-13). I rejoiced and praised God that there was such a prison to bring them to Jesus, yet I mourned that there were so many who still loved this house of bondage and would not escape, even though there stood someone with his finger always pointing to the words: *By the works of the law shall no flesh be justified* (Galatians 2:16), and to these other words: *For by grace are ye saved through faith and that not of yourselves: it is the gift of God* (Ephesians 2:8).

Chapter 2

The Only Salvation

What a great word *salvation* is! It includes the cleansing of our conscience from all past guilt and the delivery of our soul from all those inclinations to evil which so strongly work in us. In fact, it accomplishes the undoing of all that Adam did. Salvation is the total restoration of man from his fallen condition, yet it is something more than that, because God's salvation makes our standing more secure than it was before we fell. It finds us broken in pieces by the sin of our first parent – defiled, stained, accursed – and it heals our wounds. It removes our diseases, takes away our curse, and puts our feet upon the rock, Christ Jesus. Having done all this, it also lifts our heads far above all principalities and powers, to be crowned forever with Jesus Christ, the king of heaven.

Some people, when they use the word *salvation*, understand nothing more by it than deliverance from hell and admittance into heaven. That is not salvation.

Those two things are the effects of salvation. We are redeemed from hell because we are saved, and we enter heaven because we have been saved. Our everlasting state is the effect of salvation in this life. Salvation, it is true, includes all that, because salvation is the mother of it, but it would be wrong for us to think that is the entire meaning of the word.

Salvation begins with us as wandering sheep. It follows us through all our mazy wanderings. It puts us on the shoulders of the shepherd and carries us into the fold. It calls together the friends and neighbors and rejoices over us. It preserves us in that fold through life. Then, at last, it brings us to the green pastures of heaven, beside the still waters of bliss, where we lie down forever in the presence of the Chief Shepherd, never more to be disturbed.

Neither is there salvation in any other (Acts 4:12). Did you ever notice the intolerance of God's religion? In ancient times, the heathen, who had different gods, all respected the gods of their neighbors. For instance, the king of Egypt confessed that the gods of Nineveh were true and real gods, and the prince of Babylon acknowledged that the gods of the Philistines were true and real gods. But Jehovah, the God of Israel, put this as one of His first commandments: *Thou shalt have no other gods before me* (Exodus 20:3). He would not allow them to pay the slightest possible respect to the gods of any other nation: *Ye shall destroy their altars, break their images, and cut down their groves* (Exodus 34:13).

All other nations were tolerant of one another, but the Jewish people could not be so. One part of his religion was *Hear, O Israel: The LORD our God is one LORD* (Deuteronomy 6:4). As the consequence of his belief that there was only one God, Jehovah, he felt it was his duty to call all pretend gods by nicknames, to spit upon them, and to treat them with insult and contempt. The Christian religion is just as intolerant as this. If you ask a Hindu priest the way of salvation, he will very likely tell you that all people who follow their sincere religious convictions will undoubtedly be saved.

The Hindu priest might give some examples. He says that if Muslims obey Mohammed and sincerely believe what he has taught, without doubt, Allah will glorify them in the end. He will say to the Christian missionary "What is the use of bringing your Christianity here to disturb us? Our religion is quite capable of carrying us to heaven if we are faithful to it."

> There is no true salvation outside of Jesus Christ.

Now hear how intolerant the Christian religion is: *Neither is there salvation in any other* (Acts 4:12). The Hindu priest might admit that there is salvation in fifty religions besides his own, but we admit no such thing. There is no true salvation outside of Jesus Christ. The gods of the heathens may approach us with their false charity and tell us that everyone may follow his own conscientious conviction and be saved. We reply in no such way. *Neither is there salvation in any other, for there is no other name under heaven given among men in which we can be saved* (Acts 4:12).

Now, what do you suppose is the reason for this intolerance? I believe it is just because the Jew and the

Christian both hold to the truth. A thousand errors may live in peace with one another, but truth is the hammer that breaks them all in pieces. A hundred lying religions may sleep peaceably in one bed, but wherever the Christian religion goes as the truth, it is like a burning ember. It tolerates nothing that is not more substantial than the wood, the hay, and the stubble of carnal error.

All the gods of the heathen and all other religions are born of hell. Therefore, being children of the same father, it would seem wrong that they would fall out, condemn, and fight each other, but the religion of Christ is from God. Its pedigree is from on high, and therefore, when it is thrust into the midst of an ungodly generation in opposition to God's truth, it has neither peace nor compromise nor treaty with them, for it is truth, and truth cannot afford to be yoked with error. It stands upon its own rights and gives to error its due, declaring that it has no salvation except in the truth, and salvation is only to be found in the truth.

Once I thought there was salvation in good works, and I labored hard and strove diligently to safeguard my character in integrity and uprightness; but when the Spirit of God came into my heart, *sin revived, and I died* (Romans 7:9). That which I thought had been good proved to be evil, and where I thought I had been holy, I found myself to have been unholy. I discovered that my very best actions were sinful, that my tears needed to be wept over, and that my very prayers needed God's forgiveness.

I discovered that I was seeking salvation by the

works of the law and that I was doing all my good works from a selfish motive – namely, to save myself – and therefore, my works could not be acceptable to God. I found out that I could not be saved by good works for two very good reasons. First, I didn't have any. Secondly, if I had any, they could not save me.

After that, I thought that certainly salvation could be obtained partly by reformation, or changing my behavior, and partly by trusting in Christ. So I labored much again, thinking that if I added a few prayers here and there, a few tears of remorse, and a few vows of change, all would be well.

There was still an aching void in my heart that the world could never fill.

After trudging on for many weary days like a poor blind horse toiling around the mill, I found I had no improvement, because the curse of God was still hanging over me. *Cursed is every one that continues not in all things which are written in the book of the law to do them* (Galatians 3:10). There was still an aching void in my heart that the world could never fill. It was a void of distress and concern. I was very troubled because I could not achieve the rest that my soul desired.

Have you tried those two ways of getting to heaven? If you have, I trust that the Lord, the Holy Spirit, has made you thoroughly sick of them, because you will never enter the kingdom of heaven by the correct door until you have first been led to confess that all the other doors are closed to you. No one ever went to God through the strait and narrow way until he had tried all the other ways. When we find ourselves beaten, frustrated, and defeated, it is then that, pressed by pure necessity, we take ourselves to the one open fountain, where we wash ourselves and are made clean.

I will tell you that surely there must be salvation available in Christ for you, for I have found salvation in Christ for myself. I will never doubt the salvation of anyone as long as I know that Christ has accepted me. Oh, how dark my despair was when I first sought His mercy seat. I thought that even if He had mercy on the whole world, He would never have mercy on me. The sins of my childhood and of my youth haunted me. I tried to get rid of them one by one, but I was caught as in an iron net of evil habits, and I could not escape them.

Even when I could abandon my sin, the guilt still clung to my garments. I could not wash myself clean. I prayed for three long years. I bent my knees and sought Him in vain, but found no mercy. At last, blessed be His name, when I had given up all hope and thought that His swift anger would destroy me and the pit would open its mouth and swallow me up, He revealed Himself to me and taught me to cast myself simply and solely upon Him. It will be the same with you. Just trust Him, because you can be assured that there is salvation in Him.

If you do not find salvation in Christ, you will not find it anywhere. What a dreadful thing it will be for you if you miss out on the salvation provided by Christ! *How shall we escape, if we belittle such great saving health?* (Hebrews 2:3). Whether we are blatant sinners or not, how fearful a thing it will be for us to die without first having found an interest in the Savior! O sinner, this should motivate you to go to the mercy seat – that if you find no mercy at the feet of Jesus, you will not find it anywhere.

If the gates of heaven never open to you, remember there is no other gate that can ever be opened for your salvation. If Christ refuses you, you are refused. If His blood is not sprinkled on you, you are lost indeed. If He keeps you waiting a little while, still continue in prayer. It is worth waiting for, especially when you have this thought to keep you waiting – that there is none other, no other way, no other hope, no other ground of trust, no other refuge.

There I see the gate of heaven, and if I must enter it, I must crawl on my hands and knees, because it is a low gate. There I see it, it is a strait and narrow one. I must leave my sins and my proud righteousness behind me, and I must crawl in through that gate.

Come sinner, what do you say? Will you enter through this strait and narrow gate, or will you reject eternal life and refuse eternal joy? Come, sinner, and humbly go through it, trusting that He who gave Himself for you will accept you in Himself. He will save you now, and He will save you everlastingly.

Chapter 3

Those Who Do Not
Take Warning

In all worldly things, people are always awake enough to understand their own interests. There is barely a business owner who reads the paper and does not read it in some way or other with a view to his own personal concerns. If he learns that by the rise or fall of the markets he will be either a gainer or a loser, that part of the day's news will be the most important to him. In politics, in everything that concerns worldly affairs, personal interest usually leads the way. People will always look out for themselves, and personal and home interests will generally consume the majority of their thoughts.

In religion, it is otherwise. In religion, people would rather believe abstract doctrines and talk about general truths than the searching questions which examine their own personal interest in it. You will hear many people admire the preacher who deals in generalities, but when he presses searching questions and speaks about specific sins, they are offended.

If we stand and declare general facts, such as that all of us have sinned or that we all need a Savior, they will agree with our doctrine. They might even go away delighted with the discussion, because it has not affected them. But how often will our audience gnash their teeth and go away in anger, because like the Pharisees with Jesus, they perceive, concerning a faithful minister, that he spoke of *them*. How foolish this is!

If in all other matters we look to our own concerns, how much more should we do so in religion? Certainly everyone must give an account for himself at the day of judgment. We must die alone. We must rise at the day of resurrection one by one, and each one must appear before the judgment seat of God. Each one must either have said to Him, as an individual, *Come, ye blessed of my Father, inherit the kingdom prepared for you from the foundation of the world* (Matthew 25:34), or else he must be appalled with the thundering sentence, *Depart from me, ye cursed, into eternal fire, prepared for the devil and his angels* (Matthew 25:41).

If there were such a thing as national salvation, if it could be possible for us to be saved in bulk, so that like the sheaves of corn, the few weeds that happen to grow with the stubble would be gathered in for the sake of the wheat, then indeed it might not be so foolish for us to neglect our own personal interests. But if each individual sheep must pass under the hand of God, if everyone must personally and individually stand on his own before God to be tried for his own acts, then by everything that is rational, by everything that conscience would dictate and that self-interest would command, let us each look to ourselves so we will not be deceived and find ourselves miserably cast away from God forever.

A warning might be all that we could expect. If during war an army is attacked and destroyed while asleep during the night, if it had been impossible for them to have been aware of the attack and if they had used all diligence in placing their watchmen, but nevertheless the foe was so careful as to destroy them, we would weep. We would not assign blame to anyone, but we would be sad about what happened and feel compassion toward that army.

> Their blood must rest upon their own heads.

On the other hand, if they had posted their sentinels and the sentinels were wide awake and gave the sleepy soldiers every warning that could be desired, but the army was still destroyed, we would likely regret the loss of human life, but at the same time we would be compelled to say that if they were foolish enough to sleep after the sentinels had warned them, if they folded their arms in presumptuous sloth after they had had sufficient notice of the progress of their bloodthirsty enemy, then we cannot pity them in their dying. Their blood must rest upon their own heads.

It is the same with you. If people perish and have not been sufficiently warned to escape from the wrath to come, Christians may pity them even when they stand before the judgment seat of God. Although the fact that they had not been warned will not fully excuse them, it will go far to diminish their eternal miseries which otherwise might have fallen upon their heads, for we know it is more tolerable for unwarned Tyre and Sidon in the day of judgment than it is for any city or nation that has had the gospel proclaimed in its ears. *Woe unto thee, Chorazin! woe unto thee, Bethsaida! for if the mighty works which were done in you had been done in Tyre and Sidon, they would have repented long ago in sackcloth and ashes. But I say unto you, It shall be more tolerable for Tyre and Sidon at the day of judgment than for you* (Matthew 11:21-22).

He heard the sound of the shofar and did not take warning; his blood shall be upon himself. But he that takes warning shall deliver his soul (Ezekiel 33:5). In many places here and around the world, the trumpet sound of God's warning is not heard. There are multitudes of our fellow creatures who have never been warned by God's ambassadors, who do not know that wrath abides on them. *He that believes in the Son has eternal life, and he that does not obey the Son shall not see life, but the wrath of God abides on him* (John 3:36). They do not yet understand the only way and method of salvation. The trumpet was not only heard, but its warning was understood. When the man mentioned in Ezekiel 33:5 heard the sound of the trumpet, he understood that the enemy was at hand, yet he disregarded the warning.

In many of your cases, the warning has been very frequent. If the man heard the trumpet sound once and did not regard it, we might possibly excuse him, but many of you have often heard the trumpet sound of the gospel.

Young man, you have had many years of a godly mother's teaching or many years of a godly minister's exhortations. Truckloads of sermons have been exhausted on you. You have had many life-changing experiences and many terrible sicknesses. Often, when the death bell tolled for your friend, your conscience was stirred up. To you, warnings are not unusual things, but are very common.

Readers, if a person hears the gospel only once, his blood would be upon his own head for rejecting it, but how much more severe punishment will you deserve if you have heard it many, many times! I may very well weep when I think of how many sermons many of you have listened to and how many times you have been cut to the heart. You have gone up to the house of God a hundred times every year, and even more than that, and you have just added a hundred pieces of wood to the eternal fire. A hundred times the trumpet has sounded in your ears, and a hundred times you have turned away to sin again, to despise Christ, to neglect your eternal interests, and to pursue the pleasures and concerns of this world.

Oh, how foolish this is – how insane! If someone had poured out his heart to you only once concerning your eternal interests, and if he had spoken to you passionately and you had rejected his message, even then you would be guilty. But what should we say to you on whom the arrows of the Almighty have been exhausted? What will be done to this barren ground that has been watered with shower after shower and that has been nurtured with sunshine after sunshine? What will be done to him who has been rebuked repeatedly and still hardens his neck in pride and rebellion? Will he not be suddenly destroyed without remedy? *He that being often reproved hardens his neck shall suddenly be destroyed and that without remedy* (Proverbs 29:1). Won't it then be said, "His blood lies at his own door, and his guilt is on his own head"?

I ask you to remember one more thing. This warning that you have heard so often has come to you in time.

"God never considers man," an unbeliever once said. "If there is a God, He would never take notice of men."

A Christian minister who was sitting across from him said, "The day may come, sir, when you will learn the truth of what you have just said."

"I don't understand your statement, sir," the unbeliever said.

"Well, sir, the day may come, when you might call and He will refuse. You might stretch out your hands to Him, and He will not pay attention to you, but as He has said in the book of Proverbs, so He will do." *Because I have called and ye refused; I have stretched out my hand, and no one responded; for because ye have disregarded all my counsel and rejected my reproof: I also will laugh at your calamity; I will mock when your fear comes upon you* (Proverbs 1:24-26).

If you are now reading this, then your warning has not come too late. You are not being warned on a sick bed at the eleventh hour when there is little hope of salvation. You are being warned in time. You are warned today, and you have been warned for the many years that are now past. If God would send a preacher to the damned in hell, that would only add to their misery. If one could go and preach the gospel through the fields of Gehenna and tell them about a Savior they had despised and of a gospel that is now beyond their reach, that would be taunting their poor souls with a vain attempt to increase their unspeakable woe. But to preach the gospel now is to preach in a time of hope, because *now is the acceptable time; behold, now is the day of saving health* (2 Corinthians 6:2).

Warn the boatman before he enters the current, and then if he is swept down the rapids, he destroys himself. Warn the man before he drinks the cup of poison. Tell him it is deadly, and then if he drinks it, his death lies at his own door. In the same way, let us warn you before you depart this life. Let us preach to you while your bones are still full of marrow and the sinews of your joints are not loosed. We will have warned you in time, and because of this, your guilt will be increased. The warning was timely. It was frequent. It was earnest and appropriate. It was more than enough to wake you out of your sleep. It was continually given to you, and yet you still did not seek to escape from the wrath to come.

> Warn the man before he drinks the cup of poison.

Some say, "Well, I did not pay attention to the warning because I did not believe there was any need for it." You were told that there was judgment after death, and you did not believe there was any reason you should be prepared for that judgment. You were told that *by the deeds of the law, no flesh shall be justified in his sight* (Romans 3:20), and that only through Christ can sinners be saved, and you did not think there was any need for Christ. Well, you should have thought there was a need.

You knew there was a necessity in your inner consciousness. You spoke very boldly when you stood up as a professed unbeliever, but you know there was a still small voice that betrayed your tongue as you spoke. You are well aware that in the middle of the night you have often trembled. In a storm at sea, you have been on your knees to pray to a God whom on the land you have laughed at. When you have been sick and near death, you have said, "Lord, have mercy upon me." When you faced difficult circumstances, you quickly looked to the God that you earlier mocked. So you have prayed and you have believed it after all.

If you did not believe it, you should have believed it. There was enough in reason alone to have taught you that there was life after death. The Book of God's revelation was clear enough to have taught it to you, but if you have rejected God's Book and rejected the voice of reason and of conscience, your blood is on your own head. Your excuse is worthless. It is worse than that; it is profane and wicked, and your everlasting torment will be on your own head.

"But," cries another, "I did not like the trumpet. I did not like the gospel that was preached." Someone else says, "I did not like certain doctrines in the Bible. I thought the pastor preached doctrines that were too harsh sometimes. I did not agree with the gospel. I thought the gospel should have been different and not have been just what it was."

You did not like the trumpet? Well, God made the trumpet, and God made the gospel. However much you did not like what God made, it is an empty excuse. What should it matter to you what the trumpet was, as long as it warned you? Certainly, if it had been a time of war and you had heard a trumpet sounding to warn you of the coming of the enemy, you would not have sat still and said, "I believe that is a brass trumpet. I would like to have had it made of silver." No, the sound would have been enough for you, and you would have been up to escape from the danger. It must be the same with you now. It is an foolish excuse that you did not like it. You should have liked it, because God made the gospel what it is.

You say, "I did not like the man who blew the trumpet." Well, if you did not like one messenger of God, there are many others in this city. Could you not find one you did like? You did not like one man's manner because it was too theatrical. You did not like another's because it was too doctrinal. You did not like another's because it was too practical. There are plenty of people blowing the trumpet, and you can take whichever one you do like, but you make a poor excuse for each one.

If God has sent the men and told them how to blow the trumpet, and if they blow to the best of their ability, it is all in vain for you to reject their warnings because they do not blow the trumpet exactly the way you like. We do not find fault with the way a man speaks if we are in a house that is on fire. If the man calls, "Fire!

Fire!" we are not particular what tone he takes and we do not think about the harshness of his voice. You would think anyone to be a confused fool who would lie in his bed to be burned because he said he did not like the way the man yelled "Fire!" He should have been out of bed and down the stairs at once, as soon as he heard it.

Another says, "I did not like the man himself. I did not like the man who blew the trumpet. I could hear him, but I had a personal dislike for him, so I did not pay attention to the trumpet sound."

God will say to you in the end, "You fool! Why lose your soul because you did not like that man? *By his own master he stands or falls* (Romans 14:4). Your business was with yourself."

What would you think of a man who falls overboard from a ship, and as he is drowning, a sailor throws him a rope, but the man makes excuses as to why he does not grab hold of the rope?

First, he says, "I do not like that rope. I don't think that rope was made by the best manufacturer. There is some tar on it, too. I do not like it."

Next, he says, "I don't like that sailor who threw the rope over. I am sure he is not a kind-hearted man, and I don't like the look of him at all."

Then comes a gurgle and a groan, and he is down at the bottom of the sea. When he drowned, they said that it served him right. If he refused to grab hold of the rope, but instead made such foolish and absurd objections when it was a matter of life and death, then his blood was on his own head.

So shall it be with you in the end. You are so busy criticizing Christians and their doctrine, that your own soul perishes. You may be so busy criticizing the Word of God, that you never see its truth. You may get into hell by criticism, but you will never criticize your soul out of it. You may try to make the most of it. You may be there and say, "I didn't like the minister. I didn't like his manner, and I didn't like what he said," but all your dislikes will not get one drop of water to cool your burning tongue nor serve to ease the intense torments of that world of agony.

> What will you say about the man who had so much to do that he couldn't get out of the burning house?

Many other people say, "Well, I did none of those things, but I believed that the trumpet sound would be blown for everybody else, but not for me."

That is a very common notion. "All men think all men mortal but themselves," said a good poet,[1] and all people think all people need the gospel, but not themselves. Let each of us remember that the gospel has a message for each one of us.

"Well," says another, "I was so busy. I had so much to do that I couldn't possibly tend to my soul's concerns."

What will you say about the man who had so much to do that he couldn't get out of the burning house, but was burned to ashes? What will you say of the man who had so much to do, that when he was dying, he didn't have time to send for a physician?

---

1   Edward Young (1683-1765)

You will say, "Then he shouldn't have had so much to do."

If any person in the world has a business that causes him to lose his own soul for lack of time, let him pose this question to his heart: *For what is a man profited if he shall gain the whole world and lose his own soul? or what shall a man give in exchange for his soul?* (Matthew 16:26). But it is false. People do have time. It is the lack of will, not the lack of opportunity. You have time, despite all your business, to spend in pleasure. You have time to read your newspaper. Have you no time to read your Bible? You have time to listen to music. Have you no time to pray a prayer?

When farmer Brown met farmer Smith in the market one day, he said to him, "Farmer Smith, I can't understand how you find time for hunting. With all that sowing and mowing and reaping and plowing and all that, my time is so fully occupied on my farm that I have no time for hunting."

"Farmer Brown," he said, "if you liked hunting as much as I do, if you could not find time, you'd make it."

So it is with Christianity. The reason people can't find time for it is because they do not like it well enough. If they liked it, they would find time. Besides, what time does it need? What time does it require? Can I not pray to God while I am at work? Can I not read a passage of Scripture at breakfast and think over it all day? Even when I am busy in the business of the world, can I not be thinking of my soul and casting myself upon the Redeemer's blood and atonement?

Lack of time is no good excuse. There may be some

time required for my private devotions and for communion with Christ, but when I grow in grace, I will think it is right to have more and more time. The more I can possibly get, the happier I will be, and I will never make the excuse that I have no time.

"Well," says another, "I have plenty of time to follow Jesus, but you don't want me to be too religious in my youth, do you? I am still young. Can't I focus on fun now and sow my wild oats the same as anybody else?"

Well, yes, but at the same time, the best place that I know of for happiness is where a Christian lives. The greatest happiness in all the world is the happiness of a child of God. You can have your pleasures, but you will have them doubled and tripled if you are a Christian. You will not have things that those of the world call pleasures, but you will have some that are a thousand times better.

> The best place that I know of for happiness is where a Christian lives.

Consider this sorrowful picture. There, far away in the dark gulf of woe, lies a young man. He cries, "Ah, I meant to repent when I finished my apprenticeship, but I died before my time was up."

"Ah," says another by his side, "and I thought, while I was a journeyman, that when I came to be a master at my trade, I would then think of the things of Christ, but I died before I got enough money to start my own business."

Then a nearby merchant cries out with bitter woe and says, "I thought I would turn to Jesus when I had saved enough to retire on and was living in the country.

Then I would have time to think of God after all my children were out of the house and married and my concerns were settled around me, but here I am shut up in hell. What are all my delays worth now, and what is all the time I gained for all the miserable pleasures of this world? I have lost my soul over them."

We sometimes get irritated if we or others are not punctual, but we cannot conceive what must be the horror and dismay of those who find themselves too late in the next world! Friends, if I knew there was one here who said, "I will repent next Wednesday," I would wish for him to feel in a dreadful condition until that Wednesday came, because what if he would die before then? Would his promise of a Wednesday repentance save him from a Tuesday damnation?

The sinner will certainly perish, but in the end, he will perish without excuse. His blood will be on his own head. When a man is bankrupt and says, "It is not through reckless trading. It has been entirely through the dishonesty of someone I trusted that I have ended up what I am," then he takes some consolation and says, "I cannot help it."

However, if you bankrupt your own souls after you have been warned, then your own eternal bankruptcy will lie at your own door. If a great misfortune comes upon us and we can trace it to the hand of God, we bear it cheerfully; but if we have inflicted the trouble upon ourselves, then how fearful it is!

Let everyone remember that if he perishes after having heard the gospel, he will be his own murderer. Sinner, you will drive the dagger into your heart yourself. If you despise and reject the gospel, you are preparing fuel for your own bed of flames. You are hammering out the chain for your own everlasting bondage. When you are damned, your mournful reflection will be this: "I have damned myself. I cast myself into this pit, for I rejected the gospel. I despised the message. I trampled underfoot the Son of Man. I accepted none of His rebukes, and I despised His Word. I would not listen to His exhortations, and now I perish by my own hand – the miserable suicide of my own soul."

Chapter 4

How to Get Saving Faith

For by grace are ye saved through faith and that not of yourselves: it is the gift of God, not of works, lest any man should boast (Ephesians 2:8-9). Because God is gracious, sinful people are forgiven, converted, purified, and saved. It is not because of anything in them or that ever can be in them that they are saved, but it is only because of the boundless love, goodness, pity, compassion, mercy, and grace of God.

Pause a moment at the place where the spring begins. Behold the pure river of water of life as it proceeds out of the throne of God and of the Lamb (Revelation 22:1). How limitless is the grace of God! Who can comprehend it? Like all the rest of the divine attributes, it is infinite. God is full of love, for God is love (1 John 4:8). God is full of goodness, and the very name *God* is short for *good*.

Unlimited goodness and love enter into the very essence of the Godhead. It is because *His mercy endures for ever* (Psalm 136:1) that people are not destroyed. It is because His compassion never fails (Lamentations 3:22) that sinners are brought to Him and forgiven. Remember this, or you may fall into error by focusing your minds so much on the faith that is the channel of salvation that you forget the grace that is the fountain and source of faith itself.

Faith is the work of God's grace in us. No one can say that Jesus is the Christ except by the Holy Spirit (1 Corinthians 12:3). *No one can come to me unless the Father who has sent me draws him* (John 6:44); so faith, which is coming to Christ, is the result of God drawing us to Him. Grace is the first and last moving cause of salvation, and faith, as important as it is, is only an important part of the method that grace uses. We are saved *through faith*, but it is *by grace*. Proclaim those words as with the archangel's trumpet: *By grace are ye saved*.

> Faith is the channel through which the water flows, but grace is the fountain and the stream.

Faith is the channel through which the water flows, but grace is the fountain and the stream. Faith is the aqueduct along which the flood of mercy flows down to refresh the thirsty sons of men. It is a great pity when the aqueduct is broken. It is a sad sight to see!

How can we obtain and increase our faith? This is a very serious question to many. They say they want to believe, but cannot. A great deal of nonsense is spoken about this subject. Let's be practical now as we deal with it.

"What do I need to do in order to believe?"

The shortest way is simply to believe, and if the Holy Spirit has made you honest and truthful, you will believe as soon as the truth is set before you. The gospel command is clear: *Believe on the Lord Jesus Christ, and thou shalt be saved* (Acts 16:31).

If you have difficulty with this, take it before God in prayer. Tell the great Father exactly what it is that puzzles you, and ask Him by His Holy Spirit to help you. If I cannot understand a statement in a book, I am happy to inquire of the author what he meant. If he is a truthful man, his explanation will satisfy me. Even more will the divine explanation satisfy the heart of the true seeker. The Lord is willing to make Himself known. Go to Him and see that this is true.

Furthermore, if faith seems difficult, it is possible that God the Holy Spirit will enable you to believe if you hear frequently and earnestly that which you are commanded to believe. We believe many things simply because we have heard them so often. Don't you find it to be true in your life, that if you hear something fifty times a day, you often end up believing it?

Some people have come to believe things that are false by this same process. I shouldn't be surprised that God often blesses this method in working out faith concerning that which is true, for it is written, *Faith comes by hearing* (Romans 10:17). If I earnestly and attentively hear the gospel, it may be that one of these days I will find myself believing that which I hear through the work of the Spirit upon my mind.

The Samaritans believed because of what the woman told them concerning Jesus. Many of our beliefs arise out of the testimony of others. For example, I believe that there is such a country as Japan. I've never seen it, but I believe there is such a place, because others have been there. I believe I will die. I have never died, but many have done so whom I once knew. I also have a conviction that I will die. The testimony of many convinces me of this fact.

Listen, then, to those who tell you how they were saved, how they were pardoned, and how they have been changed in character. If you will just listen, you will find that somebody just like yourself has been saved. If you have been a thief, you will find that a thief washed away his sin in the fountain of Christ's blood. You who have been impure in life will find that people who have fallen that way have been cleansed and changed. If you are in despair, you only have to get among God's people and inquire a little, and some who have been equally in despair will tell you how God saved them. As you listen to one after another of those who have tried the Word of God and proved it, the divine Spirit will lead you to believe.

Haven't you heard of the African who was told by the missionary that water sometimes became so hard that a person could walk on it? He declared that he believed a great many things the missionary had told him, but he would never believe that. When he came to England, one frosty day he saw the river frozen, but he would not venture out on it. He knew that it was a river, and he was certain that he would be drowned if he ventured upon it. He could not be convinced to walk on the ice until his friend went on it. Then he was persuaded, and he trusted himself where others had gone ahead of him. So perhaps when you see others believe and notice their joy and peace, you will be gently led to believe. It is one of God's ways of helping us to faith.

An even better plan is to note the authority upon which you are commanded to believe, and this will greatly help you. The authority is not mine, or you might well reject it. It is not even the Pope's, or you might rightly reject that. You are commanded to believe on the authority of God Himself.

He asks you to believe in Jesus Christ, and you must not refuse to obey your Maker.

> God asks you to believe in Jesus Christ, and you must not refuse to obey your Maker.

The foreman of a certain factory in the north had often heard the gospel, but he was troubled with the fear that he might not be able to come to Christ. His good employer one day sent a card to him at work. It said, "Come to my house immediately after work."

The foreman arrived at his employer's door, and the employer came out and said somewhat roughly, "What do you want, John, troubling me at this hour? Work is done. What right do you have to be here?"

"Sir," he said, "I got a card from you saying that I was to come here after work."

"Do you mean to say that just because you had a card from me, you would come to my house and call me out after business hours?"

"Well, sir," replied the foreman, "I don't understand

you, but it seems to me that since you sent for me, I had a right to come."

"Come in, John," said his employer. "I have another message that I want to read to you." He sat down and read these words: *Come unto me, all ye that labour and are heavy laden, and I will give you rest* (Matthew 11:28). "Do you think after such a message from Christ that you can be wrong in going to Him?"

The poor man understood at once and believed, because he saw that he had good authority for believing. So do you, dear soul. You have good authority for coming to Christ, because the Lord Himself asks you to trust Him.

If that doesn't convince you to trust in Jesus, then consider what it is that you have to believe. The Lord Jesus Christ suffered in our place and is able to save all who trust Him. This is the most blessed fact that we were ever told to believe. This is the most suitable, the most comforting, the most divine truth that was ever set before us. I advise you to think much upon it and search out the grace and love which it contains. Study the four evangelists. Study Paul's epistles. Then see if the message is not so credible that you are forced to believe it.

If that still doesn't do it for you, then think upon the person of Jesus Christ. Think of who He is, what He did, where He is now, and what He is now. Think upon Him often and deeply. When He – the Lord and Savior Himself – instructs you to trust Him, then surely your heart will be convinced. How can you doubt Him?

If none of these things cause you to turn to Christ

Jesus, then there is something wrong about you altogether. Submit yourself to God! May the Spirit of God take away your opposition and make you yield. You are a rebel, a proud rebel, and that is why you do not believe your God. Give up your rebellion, throw down your weapons, be wise, and surrender to your King.

I believe no one ever threw up his hands in self-despair and cried, "Lord, I yield," when faith did not become easy to such a person before long. If you cannot believe, it is because you still have a quarrel with God and intend to have your own will and your own way. Christ asked, *How can ye believe, who take glory one from another, and seek not the glory that comes only from God?* (John 5:44). A proud self creates unbelief. Yield to your God, and then you will wonderfully believe in your Savior.

Chapter 5

Running for a Purpose

S ome people think they must be religious in order
to be respectable. There are a vast number of people in the world who go to church because everybody
else does. It doesn't look good not to go to church on
Sunday, so they attend the services. They think they
have done their duty and have obtained everything
that they desired when they hear their neighbors say,
"That man is a very respectable person. He is always
very regular at his church. He is a very reputable person
and worthy of praise."

If this is what you seek after in your religion, you
will get it. The Pharisees who sought the praise of others
had their reward. *Therefore, when thou doest thine alms,
do not sound a trumpet before thee, as the hypocrites
do in the synagogues and in the streets that they may
have glory of men. Verily I say unto you, They already
have their reward* (Matthew 6:2). But when you have
gotten it, what a poor reward it is! Is it worth the effort?

I don't believe that the effort people take in order to be called respectable is worth the trouble at all. I am sure, for my own part, I wouldn't care one bit what I was called or what people thought of me, nor would I do anything that was disagreeable to me for the sake of pleasing any man who ever walked beneath the stars, however great or mighty he may be. It is the sign of a groveling, squirming spirit, when people always seek to do that which causes them to appear respectable. The esteem of others is not worth pursuing, and it is sad that this is the only prize which some people pursue in the poor religion which they practice.

Loaves and fishes attracted some of Christ's followers, and they continue to attract many, even to this day.

Another set of people pursue the religious life for what they can get from it. I have known businessmen who attended church for the mere sake of getting the business of those who went there. I have heard of such things as people knowing on which side their bread was buttered, and going to a particular denomination where they thought they could get the most by it.

Loaves and fishes attracted some of Christ's followers, and they continue to attract many, even to this day. People find there is something to be gotten by religion. Among the poor it might be some little charity to be obtained, and among those who are in business, it is the business they think they will get. *Verily I say unto you, They already have their reward,* because the church is foolish and unsuspicious. We do not like to suspect our fellow creatures of following us from impure motives. The church does not like to think that someone would be corrupt enough to pretend to practice Christianity for the mere sake of what he can get.

Therefore, we let these people easily slip through, and they have their reward. But, oh, at what a price they buy it! They have deceived the Lord's servants for gold, and they have entered into His church as hypocrites for the sake of a piece of bread. They will be cast out at the end with the anger of God behind them, like Adam driven out of Eden, with the flaming sword of the cherubim turning every way to watch over the tree of life. They will forever look back upon this as the most fearful crime they have committed – that they pretended to be God's people when they were not, and that they entered into the midst of the fold when they were really wolves in sheep's clothing.

There is still another class of people, and when I have referred to them, I will mention them no more. These are the people who participate in Christianity for the sake of quieting their conscience. It is astonishing how such a little amount of religion will sometimes do that. Some people tell us that if in the time of storm, we would pour bottles of oil upon the waves, there would be a great calm at once. I have never tried it, and it is likely that I never will, because my gullibility isn't large enough to accept such a wide statement. But there are some people who think that they can calm the storm of a troubled conscience by pouring a little of the oil of a profession of faith upon it. It is amazing how significant an effect this really has.

I knew a man who got drunk many times a week and who got his money dishonestly, yet he kept his conscience at ease by regularly going to his church on Sunday. We have heard of a lawyer who could swallow up everything that came his way. He did not mind crushing the poor or portraying a guilty person as innocent, as long as he got his money; yet he never went to bed without saying his prayers, and that stilled his conscience. We have heard of other people, especially among the Romanists, who did not mind stealing or getting drunk or being immoral or taking God's name in vain, but who considered eating anything but fish on a Friday as a most fearful sin. They supposed that by fasting on Friday, all the sins of the rest of the week would be forgotten.

They want the outward forms of religion to keep their conscience quiet, because conscience is one of the worst guests to have in your house when he gets quarrelsome. There is no living with him. A guilty conscience is one of the curses of the world. It puts out the sun and takes away the brightness from the moonbeam. A guilty conscience casts an unpleasant smell through the air, removes the beauty from the landscape, the glory from the flowing river, and the majesty from the rolling floods. There is nothing beautiful to the person who has a guilty conscience. He needs no accusing, because everything accuses him. For this reason, people go through the motions of Christianity just to quiet these accusers.

They take the sacrament sometimes. They go to a place of worship. They listen to some Christian music now and then. They give a little money to a charity. They even intend to leave a portion in their will to build houses for the poor, and in this way their conscience is lulled asleep. They soothe it with religious observances, until it sleeps while they sing the lullaby of hypocrisy. Conscience doesn't wake until he wakes with that rich man who, in this life, was clothed in purple, but in the next world he lifted up his eyes in hell, being in torment, without a drop of water to cool his burning tongue. *And he cried and said, Father Abraham, have mercy on me and send Lazarus that he may dip the tip of his finger in water and cool my tongue; for I am tormented in this flame* (Luke 16:24).

The apostle Paul says, *Know ye not that those who run in a race indeed all run, but one receives the prize? So run, that ye may obtain it* (1 Corinthians 9:24). There are some people who certainly never will obtain the prize, because they are not even entered in the race. Therefore, it is quite clear that they will not run, or if they do run, they will run without having any justification for expecting to receive the prize.

There are some who will tell you themselves, "We make no profession of faith – none whatsoever." It is probably just as well that they don't, because if they did, they would be hypocrites, and it is better to make no profession at all than to be hypocrites. Still, remember that their names are not written down for the race, and therefore they cannot win. If someone tells you in business that he makes no profession of being honest, you know that he is a confirmed dishonest person. If a person makes no profession of being a Christian, you know that he is not a Christian. He has no fear of God before his eyes, he has no love for Christ, and he has no hope of heaven. He confesses it himself.

It is strange that people should be so ready to confess this. You don't find people in the street willing to acknowledge that they are confirmed drunkards. Generally, they will deny it with contempt. You never find anyone saying to you, "I am morally impure." You don't hear someone else say, "I am just a covetous fool." No. People are not so fast to tell their faults, yet they confess the greatest fault to which anyone can be addicted. They say, "I make no claim to be a Christian." This just means that they do not give God His due.

God has made them, but they won't serve Him. Christ has come into the world to save sinners, and they will not acknowledge Him. The gospel is preached, but they will not hear it. They have the Bible in their houses, but they will not pay attention to its admonitions. They make no profession of doing so. It will not take long for them at the last great day. There will be no need for the books to be opened and no need for a long deliberation for the verdict. They do not profess to be pardoned. Their guilt is written upon their own foreheads, and their brazen shamelessness will be seen by the whole world as a sentence of destruction written upon their very brows.

You cannot expect to win heaven unless your names are entered for the race. If there are no attempts made, if you do not even make an attempt to pretend to be a Christian, then you can just sit down and say, "Heaven is not for me. I have no part or lot in the inheritance of

Israel. I cannot say that my Redeemer lives, and I can
rest quite assured that hell is prepared for me from long
ago. I will feel its pains and know its miseries, because
there are only two places to dwell in the afterlife, and
if I am not found on the right hand of the Judge, there
is only one alternative – to be cast away forever into
the blackness of darkness."

Then there is another class of people whose names
are down for entering the race, but they never started
right. A bad start is a sad thing. If in the ancient races
of Greece or Rome a man who
was to run the race had started
ahead of time, it wouldn't matter
how fast he ran, for he would be
disqualified. The flag must drop
before the horse starts. Otherwise, even if it reaches
the finish line first, it will receive no reward. So there
is something to be observed in the starting of the race.
I have known men who run the race of religion with
all their might, but they lost the race because they did
not start right.

You ask, "Well, how is that?"

There are some people who try to suddenly leap into
religion. They get it quickly and they keep it for a while,
but in the end they lose it because they did not get it
the right way. They have heard that before someone
can be saved, it is necessary that, by the teaching of
the Holy Spirit, he should feel the weight of sin, that he
should make a confession of it, that he should renounce
all hope in his own works, and that he should look to
Jesus Christ alone. They look upon all these things as

> There are only two
> places to dwell in
> the afterlife.

unpleasant preliminaries. Therefore, before they have devoted themselves to repentance, before the Holy Spirit has performed a good work in them, before they have been brought to give up everything and trust in Christ, they make a profession of faith.

This often happens in our churches, when people walk down the aisle and say a prayer and think they are saved, but they have never felt the burden of sin or the necessity of true repentance. This is just opening an empty store without any merchandise, and there will be failure. If a man has nothing to begin with, he might make a fine show for a little while, but it will just be like the crackling of thorns under a pot; there will be a lot of noise and a lot of light for a little while, but it will die out in darkness. There are many who never think it necessary that there should be a work of God in their heart!

Again, there are some runners in the heavenly race who cannot win because they carry too much weight. A light weight, of course, has the advantage. There are some people who have an immensely heavy weight to carry. *Then said Jesus unto his disciples, Verily I say unto you, It is difficult that a rich man shall enter into the kingdom of the heavens* (Matthew 19:23). What is the reason? Because he carries so much weight. He has so much of the cares and pleasures of this world. He has such a heavy burden that he is not likely to win unless God gives him a mighty mass of strength to enable him to bear it.

We find many people who say they are willing to be saved. They receive the Word with great joy, but after a while, thorns spring up and choke the Word. They have so much business to do. They say they must live, but they forget they must die. They have so much business to attend to, they cannot think of living near to Christ. They find they have little time for devotions. Morning prayer must be cut short because their business begins early. They have no time or strength to pray at night, because business and other events keep them so late. How can they be expected to think of the things of God?

They have so much to do to answer these questions: What shall I eat? What shall I drink? And what shall I wear? They read in the Bible that their Father who is in heaven will take care of them in these things if they will trust Him, but they say, "Not so." They believe that those who rely solely upon God to supply those needs are overzealous fanatics. They say that the best provider in all the world is hard work, and they are correct; but they forget that *Unless the LORD builds the house, they labour in vain that build it; unless the LORD keeps the city, the watchmen watch in vain. It is vain for you to rise up early, to come home late, to eat the bread of sorrows, because he shall give his beloved sleep* (Psalm 127:1-2).

You see two men running a race. One of them lays aside every weight as he starts. He takes off his coat and away he runs. The other poor fellow has a whole load of gold and silver upon his back. Then around his loins he has many distrustful doubts about what will become of him in the future, what will happen to him when he grows old, and a hundred other things. He does not know how to place his burden upon the

Lord. See how he grows weary, poor fellow, and how the other runner leaves him far behind, has turned the corner, and is coming to the finish line.

It is good if we can cast everything away except that one thing needful and say, "My main business on earth is to serve God, knowing that I will enjoy Him in heaven." When we leave our business to God, we leave it in better hands than if we took care of it ourselves. Those who carve for themselves generally cut their fingers, but those who allow God to carve for them will never have an empty plate. He who follows after a cloud will go in the right direction, but he who runs in front of it will soon find that he has gone on a fool's errand. *Blessed is the man that is steadfast in the LORD and whose trust is the LORD* (Jeremiah 17:7). *The young lions do lack and suffer hunger, but those that seek the LORD shall not lack any good thing* (Psalm 34:10).

Our Savior said, *Behold the fowls of the air, for they sow not, neither do they reap nor gather into barns, yet your heavenly Father feeds them. Are ye not much better than they? Which of you by taking thought can add one cubit unto his stature? And why take ye thought for raiment? Consider the lilies of the field, how they grow: they toil not, neither do they spin; and yet I say unto you, That even Solomon in all his glory was not arrayed like one of these* (Matthew 6:26-29).

We can safely trust in the God of Israel. *He shall dwell upon the high places: fortresses of rocks shall be his place of refuge: bread shall be given him; his waters shall be sure* (Isaiah 33:16). *But seek ye first the kingdom of God and his righteousness, and all these things shall be added unto you* (Matthew 6:33).

If you carry the weight of this world's cares upon you, it will be as much as you can do to carry them and to stand upright under them; but running a race with such burdens is just impossible.

It is good when you sail over the smooth waters of life, but the rough billows of the Jordan will make you want a Savior. It is hard work to die without a hope, and to take that last leap in the dark is a frightful thing indeed. I have seen the old man die when he has declared that he would not die. He stood upon the brink of death and said, "All dark, dark, dark! O God, I cannot die." His agony has been fearful when the strong hand of the destroyer seemed to push him over the precipice. He "lingered shivering on the brink, and feared to launch away."[2] Frightful was the moment when his foot slipped, he left the solid earth, and his soul was sinking into the depths of eternal wrath.

> It is hard work to die without a hope, and to take that last leap in the dark is a frightful thing indeed.

You will want a Savior then, when your pulse is faint and few. You will need an angel to stand at your bedside, and when the spirit is departing, you will need a sacred convoy to pilot you through the dark clouds of death, guide you through the iron gate, and lead you to the blessed mansion in the land of the hereafter. *Seek the LORD while he may be found; call upon him while he is near: Let the wicked forsake his way, and the unrighteous*

---

2   From Isaac Watts' hymn "There Is a Land of Pure Delight."

man his thoughts: and let him return unto the LORD, and he will have mercy upon him; and to our God, for he will abundantly pardon. For my thoughts are not as your thoughts, neither are your ways as my ways, saith the LORD. For as the heavens are higher than the earth, so are my ways higher than your ways, and my thoughts more than your thoughts (Isaiah 55:6-9). O Lord, turn us and we will be turned. *Turn us unto thee, O LORD, and we shall be turned* (Lamentations 5:21). Draw us near and we will run after You. The glory will be yours, for the crown of our race will be cast at Your feet, and You will have the glory forever and ever.

Chapter 6

The Course of the Wicked

It is quite certain that there are immense benefits in our present mode of burying the dead outside of church grounds. It is high time that the dead should be removed from the midst of the living – that we should not worship in the midst of corpses and sit in the Lord's house on the Sabbath breathing the noxious odor of decaying bodies. We must remember, though, that there are some advantages that we have lost by the removal of the dead from our immediate proximity, and more especially by the wholesale mode of burial which now seems very likely to become common. We are no longer commonly met by the display of the dead. In the midst of our crowded cities, we sometimes see the black hearse carrying the bodies of the dead to their final resting places, but funeral ceremonies and the places where the bodies of those who are very dear to us rest are now mostly confined to those places outside of our daily view.

I believe the sight of a funeral is a very healthy thing for the soul. Whatever harm that could possibly come to the body by walking through the vault and the catacomb, the soul can find much food for contemplation and much excitement for thought. In the great villages, where some of us used to dwell, we remember how, when the funeral came now and then, the tolling of the bell preached to all the villagers a better sermon than they had heard in the church for many weeks. We remember, as children, how we used to gather around the grave and look at that which was not so frequent an occurrence in the midst of such a small population. We remember the solemn thoughts which used to arise even in our young hearts when we heard the words uttered, "Earth to earth, ashes to ashes, dust to dust."

The solemn falling of the few grains of ashes upon the coffin lid was the sowing of good seed in our hearts. Afterwards, when we, in our childish play, climbed over those nettle-bound graves and sat upon those moss-grown tombstones, we had many lessons preached to us by the dull, cold tongue of death, more eloquent than anything we had heard from the lips of living men, and more likely to stay with us for years to come. Now, however, we see little of death. We have fulfilled Abraham's wish beyond what he desired – we bury the dead out of our sight. *I am a stranger and a sojourner with you; give me a possession of a buryingplace with you, that I may bury my dead out of my sight* (Genesis 23:4). It is seldom that we see them, and a stranger passing through our streets might say, "Do these people live forever? I see no funerals among the millions of this city, and I see no signs of death."

Will we just take the wicked man's arm and walk with him to the house of God? When he begins to go, especially if he has not gone to church as a youth, you will notice that whenever he does begin to go, he is not often affected by the sound of the ministry. He goes up to the chapel with lack of respect and lack of seriousness. He approaches it as he would a theater or any other place of amusement – as a means of passing away the Lord's Day and killing time.

He walks cheerfully into the church, but I have seen the wicked man look very different when he went away than when he entered. He walks home, and his lack of respect and lack of seriousness are gone. He says, "Surely the Lord God was in that place, and I have been forced to tremble. I

> "The services of God's house are not all dullness after all."

went to scoff, but as I left, I was compelled to confess that there is a power in Christianity, and the services of God's house are not all dullness after all."

Perhaps you have hoped that spiritual good would come to this man, but sadly, he forgot it all and cast away those thoughts that were working on his soul. He came again the next Sunday, and that time he felt it again. Again, the arrow of the Lord seemed to stick securely in his heart, but it was like the rushing of water. There was a mark for a moment, but his heart was soon healed and he no longer felt the blow. As for persuading him to salvation, he was like the deaf adder: *Their*

*poison is like the poison of a serpent; they are like the
deaf adder that stops her ear, which will not hearken to
the voice of charmers, charming never so wisely* (Psalm
58:4-5). No matter what was said, he would not regard
the truth and would not turn from his ways.

I have seen him come and go until he has become
an old man, and he has still filled his seat at church.
The minister is still preaching, but in his case, preaching in vain. The tears of mercy are still flowing for him
and the thunders of justice are still launched against
him, but he remains just as he was. There is no change
in him except that he has grown hard and callous. You
no longer hear him say that he trembles under the
Word. He is like a horse that has been in the battle.
He does not fear the noise of the drum or the rolling
of the smoke, and he is not afraid of the blast of the
cannon. He shows up and he hears a faithful warning
and says, "What of it? This is for the wicked." He hears
an affectionate invitation and he says, "Go away. When
it is a more convenient time, I will send for you." So
he comes and goes up to the house of God and back
again. Like the door upon its hinges, he turns in to the
sanctuary today and out of it tomorrow. He comes and
goes from the place of the holy.

It may be, however, that he takes it even further.
Almost persuaded to be a Christian by some sermon
from someone like Paul, he trembles at his feet. He
thinks he really repents, and he unites himself with the
Christian church. He makes a profession of faith, but
his heart has never been changed. The sow is washed,
but it is still a sow. The dog has been driven from its

vomit, but its doggish nature is still the same. *It has happened unto them according to the true proverb, The dog returns unto his own vomit, and the sow that was washed to her wallowing in the mire* (2 Peter 2:22). The Ethiopian is clothed in a white garment, but he has not changed his skin. The leopard has been completely covered, but he has not washed his spots away. *Can the Ethiopian change his skin or the leopard his spots?* (Jeremiah 13:23).

The man is the same as he ever was. He goes to the baptismal pool a blind sinner, and he comes out of it the same. He goes to the table of the Lord a deceiver; he eats the bread and drinks the wine, and he returns the same. The bread of the Lord's Supper is broken in his presence. He receives it, but he comes and he goes the same, because he does not receive it in the love of it. He is a stranger to true godliness, and as a wicked man, he comes and he goes from the place of the holy.

Is it not an unbelievable thing that people are be able to do this? I have sometimes heard preachers so earnestly present the matter of salvation before the people that I have said, "Surely, they must see this." I have heard them plead as though they pleaded for their own lives and I have said, "Surely, they must feel this." I have turned around and I have seen the people wiping away tears and I have said, "Good must come from this. These people will be saved."

You have brought your own friends to hear the Word, and you have prayed through the whole sermon that the arrow might reach and penetrate the center of the mark, and you said to yourself, "What an appropriate message." You kept on praying and were pleased to see that there was some emotion. You said, "Oh, it will touch his heart at last!" But isn't it strange that, though pursued by love divine, the heart of man will not melt? Even though they are thundered at by Sinai's own terrific thunderbolts, they will not tremble. Even if Christ Himself, incarnate in the flesh, preached again, they would still not believe Him. They might even treat Him today as their ancestors did so long ago, when they dragged Him out of the city and would have thrown Him headlong from the summit of the mount on which the city was built.

I have seen the wicked come and go from the place of the holy until his conscience was seared as with a hot iron. I have seen him come and go from the place of the holy until his heart was harder than a lower millstone, until he was past feeling, and he gave himself over *unto lasciviousness to work all uncleanness with greediness* (Ephesians 4:19).

Now we are going to change our course. Instead of going to the house of God, we will go a different route. I have seen the wicked go to the place of the holy – that is, to the judgment bench. We have had glaring instances, even in the criminal justice system, of people who have been seen sitting as a judge one day, and in a short time they have been standing on the other side of that bench, as prisoners themselves.

I have wondered what the distinct feelings of a man must be who officiates as a judge, knowing that he who judges has been a lawbreaker himself. A wicked person, a greedy, lustful, drunken person – you know such will be found among some judges. We have known that these people sit and condemn the drunkard, when if the world had known how they went to bed the night before, they would have said of them, "You who judge another do the same things yourself." *Therefore, thou art inexcusable, O man, whosoever thou art that judgest; for in that which thou dost judge another, thou dost condemn thyself; for thou that judgest others doest the same things* (Romans 2:1).

There have been instances of judges who have condemned a common fellow for shooting a rabbit or stealing a few pheasant eggs, or some crime like that, while they themselves have been robbing the coffers of the bank, embezzling funds to an extreme extent, and cheating people. It must be a very strange emotion that passes over someone when he executes the law upon one person that he knows ought to be executed upon himself.

I have seen the wicked come and go from the holy place until he thinks that his sins are not really sins. He believes that the poor must be severely punished for their iniquities, that what he calls the lower classes must be kept in check, not thinking that there are none so low as those who condemn others while they do the same things themselves. He speaks about checks and restraints, when neither check nor restraint were of any use to him. He talks of cracking down on others and of judging righteously, but if righteous judgment had been carried out to the letter, he would have been the prisoner instead of being honored with a commission from the government.

I have seen the wicked man buried in a quiet way. He is taken quietly to his tomb with as little pomp as possible, and with all decency and solemnity he is interred in the grave. Now, listen to the minister. If he is a man of God, when he buries such a person as he ought to be buried, you do not hear a single word about the character of the deceased. You hear nothing at all about any hope of everlasting life. He is just put into his grave. The minister remembers well how he came and went from church. He remembers well how he used to sit in the pew and listen to his sermon. There is one who weeps, and the minister stands there and weeps, too, thinking how all his labor has been lost and how one of his hearers has been lost eternally and is now without hope.

Note how cautiously he speaks, even to the wife. He would like to give her all the hope he can, poor widow as she is, and he speaks very gently. She says, "I hope my husband is in heaven." He holds his tongue. He stays silent. If he is of a sympathetic nature, he will be quiet. When he speaks about the deceased in his next Sunday's sermon, if he mentions him at all, he refers to him as a doubtful case. He uses him as a warning rather than as an example, and urges others to consider how they carelessly waste their opportunities and disregard the golden hours of their Sabbath day.

Then I also saw that the wicked who were buried came into remembrance more than those who had frequented the holy place (Ecclesiastes 8:10). As for the pompous funeral, that was ridiculous. We might almost laugh to see the foolishness of honoring someone who deserved to be dishonored, but as for the still and silent and truthful funeral, how sad it is! After all, we should judge ourselves in the light of our funerals. That is the way we judge other things.

Look at your fields tomorrow. There is a flaunting flower, and there by the hedgerows are many flowers that lift their heads to the sun. Judging them by their leaf, you might prefer them to the sober-colored wheat. But wait until the funeral, when the flower is gathered and the weeds are bound up in a bundle to be burned. They are gathered into a heap in the field to be consumed, to be made into manure for the soil. But the wheat sheaf has a magnificent funeral. "The harvest has come!" is shouted as the wheat is carried to the storage building, for it is a precious thing.

> Let each of us live in such a way that we are constantly considering that we must die.

Let each of us live in such a way that we are constantly considering that we must die. I desire to live so that when I leave this earthly condition, people will say, "There goes one who sought to make the world better! However rough his efforts might have been, he was an honest man. He sought to serve God, and there lies he who feared not the face of man." My desire would be to have every Christian seek to deserve a funeral like Stephen's: *And devout men carried Stephen to his burial and made great lamentation over him* (Acts 8:2).

Everyone seems to want to live a little longer than his life. There is scarcely a rock to be found in all of England, up which even a goat might barely climb, where there cannot be discovered the initials of the names of people who never had any other method of attaining to fame, so they thought they would inscribe their names there. Go where you will, and you find people attempting to be known. This is the reason why many people write in newspapers, or else they would never be known. We have a hundred little inventions for keeping our names going after we are dead; but with the wicked, it is all in vain. He will be forgotten. He has done nothing to make anybody remember him.

Ask the poor, "Do you remember So-and-so?"

"He was very difficult to work for. He was not kind, and he always cut us down to the last cent, and we do not wish to remember him."

Their children will not hear his name; they will forget him entirely.

Ask the church, "Do you remember So-and-so? He was a member."

"Well," says one, "I certainly remember him. His name was on the books as being a member, but we never had his heart. He used to come and go, but I never could talk with him. There was nothing spiritual in him. He loved to talk about work and sports and politics, but not of the Scriptures and of Jesus. There was a great deal of sounding-bell metal and brass, but no gold. I never could discover that he had the foundation of Christ in him."

No one thinks about him, and he will soon be forgotten. The chapel grows old, and there another congregation arises, but they talk about the good and holy men who used to be deacons there, about the old lady who used to be so eminently useful in visiting the sick, and about the young man who rose out of that church and was so useful in the cause of God; but you never hear mention made of *his* name, for he is quite forgotten.

When he died, his name was struck out of the books. He was reported as being dead, and all remembrance of him died with him. I have often noticed how soon wicked things die when the man dies who originated them. Look at Voltaire's philosophy. With all the noise it made in his time, where is it now? There is just a little of it lingering, but it seems to have gone. There was Tom Paine, who did his best to write his name in letters of damnation. One would think he might have been remembered, but who cares about him now? Except among a few here and there, his name has passed away. All the names of error, heresy, and schism, where do they go? You hear about Augustine to this day, but you never hear about the heretics he attacked. Everybody should know about Athanasius and how he stood up for the divinity of the Lord Jesus Christ, but we have almost forgotten the life of Arius, and barely ever think of those men who aided and abetted him in his folly. Bad men die out quickly, for the world feels it is a good thing to be rid of them. They are not worth remembering.

Chapter 7

Coming to Christ

Coming to Christ is a very common phrase in Holy Scripture. It is used to express the acts of the soul where we leave our self-righteousness and our sins at once and we fly to the Lord Jesus Christ, receiving His righteousness as our covering and His blood as our atonement. Coming to Christ embraces in it repentance, self-denial, and faith in the Lord Jesus Christ. It sums up within itself all the things that are the necessary attendants of these great states of heart, such as the belief of the truth, earnestness of prayer to God, the submission of the soul to the precepts of God's gospel, and all those things that accompany the dawn of salvation in the soul. Coming to Christ is the one essential thing for a sinner's salvation. He who does not come to Christ, no matter what else he does or says, is still in *the gall of bitterness and in the prison of iniquity* (Acts 8:23).

Coming to Christ is the very first effect of regeneration.

As soon as the soul is awakened, it immediately discovers its lost condition and is horrified at that fact. It then looks for a refuge, and believing Christ to be a suitable one, flies to Him and rests in Him. Where there is not this coming to Christ, it is certain there is still no awakening. Where there is no awakening, the soul is dead in trespasses and sins. Being dead, it cannot enter into the kingdom of heaven. *No one can come to me unless the Father who has sent me draws him* (John 6:44).

Where does this inability lie?

First, it does not lie in any physical defect. If moving the body or walking with the feet were of any assistance in coming to Christ, certainly we have the physical power to come to Christ in that sense. I remember hearing a very foolish Antinomian declare that he did not believe that anyone had the power to walk to the house of God unless the Father drew him. That man was just foolish. He could plainly see that as long as a man was alive and had legs, it was as easy for him to walk to the house of God as to the house of Satan.

If coming to Christ includes the utterance of a prayer, we have no physical defect in that respect. If a person is not mute, he can say a prayer as easily as he can utter blasphemy. It is as easy for someone to sing one of the songs of Zion as it is to sing a profane and obscene song. There is no lack of physical power in coming to Christ. All that can be needed with regard to bodily strength, man most assuredly has, and any part of salvation that consists in that is totally and entirely in the power of man without any assistance from the Spirit of God.

This inability to come to Christ on our own does not lie in any mental lack. I can believe the Bible is true just as easily as I can believe any other book to be true. As far as believing on Christ is an act of the mind, I am just as able to believe on Christ as I am able to believe on anybody else. If his statement is true, it is pointless to tell me I cannot believe it. I can believe the statement that Christ makes as well as I can believe the statement of any other person.

> This inability to come to Christ on our own does not lie in any mental lack.

There is no deficiency in the mind. It is as capable of appreciating the guilt of sin as a mere mental act as it is of appreciating the guilt of assassination. It is just as possible for me to exercise the mental idea of seeking God as it is to exercise the thought of pride. I have all the mental strength and power that can possibly be needed, as far as mental power is needed in salvation at all. No, there isn't anyone so ignorant that he can plead a lack of intellect as an excuse for rejecting the gospel.

The defect, then, does not lie either in the body or in what we are bound, theologically, to call the mind. It is not any lack or deficiency of the mind, although it is the corruption or the ruin of the mind that is the very essence of man's inability.

Through the fall and through our own sin, the nature of man has become so debased, depraved, and corrupt, that it is impossible for him to come to Christ without the assistance of God the Holy Spirit. Now, in trying to explain how the nature of man renders him unable to come to Christ, consider this illustration. You see a sheep. How willingly it feeds upon the vegetation! You've never seen a sheep desire meat. It could not live on lion's food. Now bring me a wolf. Ask me whether a wolf can eat grass and whether it can be just as docile and as domesticated as the sheep. I answer no, because its nature is contrary to that.

You say, "Well, it has ears and legs. Can't it hear the shepherd's voice and follow him wherever he leads it?"

Certainly. There is no physical reason why it cannot do so, but its nature forbids it. Therefore, I say it *cannot* do so. Can't it be tamed? Can't its ferocity be removed? It could probably be subdued to the point that it appears tame, but there will always be a marked distinction between it and the sheep, because there is a distinction in nature.

The reason why man cannot come to Christ is not because he cannot come as far as his body or his mere power of mind is concerned, but because his nature is so corrupt that he has neither the will nor the power to come to Christ unless drawn by the Spirit.

Let me give you a better illustration. You see a mother with her baby in her arms. You put a knife into her hand and tell her to stab that baby in the heart.

She replies very truthfully, "I cannot."

As far as her bodily power is concerned, she can, if she wants to. There is the knife, and there is the child. The child cannot resist, and the mother has quite sufficient strength in her hand to stab its heart; but she is quite correct when she says she cannot do it. As a mere act of the mind, it is quite possible she might think of such a thing as killing the child, and yet she says she cannot think of such a thing as killing the child. She is telling the truth, because her nature as a mother forbids her to do something from which her soul revolts. Simply because she is that child's parent, she feels she cannot kill the baby.

It is the same with a sinner. Coming to Christ is so obnoxious to human nature that as far as physical and mental forces are concerned (and these have but a very limited place in salvation), people could come if they would want to. It is strictly correct to say that they cannot and will not unless the Father who has sent Christ draws them.

Man is by nature blind within. The cross of Christ, so laden with glories and glittering with attractions, never attracts him, because he is blind and cannot see its beauties. Talk to him of the wonders of creation, show him the rainbow that spans the sky, and let him behold the glories of a landscape; he is fully able to see all these things. But if you talk to him about the wonders of the covenant of grace, speak to him of the security of the believer in Christ, and tell him of the beauties of the person of the Redeemer, he is quite deaf to all that you say. You are like one who plays a pleasant tune, but he doesn't regard your music. He is deaf and has no comprehension.

Do you find your power equal to your will? You could say, even at the throne of God Himself, that you are sure you are not mistaken in your willingness. You are willing to be devoted to God. It is your will that your soul should not wander from a pure contemplation of the Lord Jesus Christ, but you find that you cannot do that, even when you are willing, without the help of the Spirit. If the awakened child of God finds a spiritual inability, how much more the sinner who is dead in trespasses and sin? If even the advanced Christian, after thirty or forty years, finds himself sometimes willing and yet powerless, does it not seem more than likely that the poor sinner who has not yet believed would find a need for strength as well as a lack of will?

There is another argument. If the sinner has strength to come to Christ, I would like to know how we are supposed to understand those continual descriptions of the sinner's condition that we find in God's Holy Word. A sinner is said to be dead in trespasses and sins (Ephesians 2:1). Will you agree that death implies nothing more than the absence of a will?

"Surely a corpse is quite unable as well as unwilling," says one. "So then, if I cannot save myself and cannot come to Christ, I must sit still and do nothing."

If people say this, their doom will be on their own heads. There are many things you can do. To be found continually in the house of God is in your power. To study the Word of God with diligence is in your power. To renounce your outward sin, to forsake the vices in which you indulge, to reform your life outwardly, is all within your power. You do not need help from the Holy Spirit for this – all this you can do yourself; but to truly come to Christ is not in your power until you are renewed by the Holy Spirit.

Your lack of power is no excuse when you have no

desire to come and are living in willful rebellion against God. Your lack of power lies mainly in your stubborn nature. Suppose a liar says that it is not in his power to speak the truth, that he has been a liar so long that he cannot stop. Is that an excuse for him? Suppose a man who has indulged in lust for a long time tells you that he finds his lusts have so enveloped him like a great iron net that he cannot get rid of them. Would you accept that as an excuse? Truly it isn't one at all. If a drunkard has become such a drunkard that he finds it impossible to pass a drinking establishment without stepping in, do you excuse him? No, because his inability to change lies in his nature, which he has no desire to restrain or conquer.

> Your lack of power lies mainly in your stubborn nature.

The thing that is done and the thing that causes the thing that is done both proceed from the root of sin. They are two evils which cannot excuse each other. So what if the Ethiopian cannot change his skin, or the leopard his spots? It is because you have learned to do evil that you cannot now learn to do what is right. Instead of letting you sit down and make excuses, let me put a thunderbolt beneath the seat of your apathy, so you may be startled and aroused by it. Remember that to sit still is to be damned for all eternity.

We tie up all our ends now and conclude by trying to make a practical application of the doctrine, and we hope it is an agreeable one. "Well," someone says, "if what this man teaches is true, what is to become of my religion? You know I have been trying for a long time, and I do not like to hear you say a man cannot save himself. I believe he can, and I intend to persevere. If I am to believe what you say, I must give it all up and begin again."

It will be a very good thing if you do. Remember, what you are doing now is building your house upon the sand, and it is even an act of love if I shake your house a little for you. Let me assure you, in God's name, if your religion has no better foundation than your own strength, it will not be good enough for you at the throne of God. Nothing will last to eternity except that which came from eternity. Unless the everlasting God has done a good work in your heart, all you have done must fall apart at the last day.

It is all in vain for you to be a faithful church attender or to be religious and regularly say your prayers. It is all in vain for you to be honest with your neighbors and reputable in your life if you hope to be saved by these things. It is all in vain for you to trust in them. Go on and be as honest as you like, keep the Lord's Day always, and be as holy as you can. I would not dissuade you from these things. God forbid! Grow in them, but do not trust in them. If you rely upon these things, you will find that they will fail you when you need them most. If there is anything else that you have found yourself unable to do unless aided by divine grace, the sooner you can get rid of the hope that has been generated by it, the better it is for you, for it is a wicked delusion to rely upon anything that flesh can do. A spiritual heaven must be inhabited by spiritual people, and preparation for it must be performed by the Spirit of God.

"Well," cries another, "I have been sitting under a ministry where I have been told that I could, whenever I decided, repent and believe, and the consequence is that I have been putting it off from day to day. I thought I could come one day as well as another, that I had only to say, 'Lord, have mercy upon me,' and believe, and then I would be saved. I thought I simply had to make a decision to believe. Now you have taken all this hope away from me. I feel amazement and horror taking hold of me."

I am very glad. This was the effect I had hoped to produce, and I pray that you feel this a great deal more. When you have no hope of saving yourself, I will have hope that God has begun to save you. As soon as you say, "Oh, I cannot come to Christ. Lord, draw me; help me," I will rejoice over you. He who has the will, even though he has not power, has the beginnings of grace in his heart, and God will not leave him until the work is finished.

However, careless sinner, learn that your salvation now hangs in God's hand. Remember that you are entirely in the hand of God! You have sinned against Him, and if He wills to damn you, you are damned. You cannot resist His will or prevent His purpose. You have deserved His wrath, and if He chooses to pour the full shower of that wrath upon your head, you can do nothing to prevent it.

If, on the other hand, He chooses to save you, He is able to save you completely; but you lie as much in His hand as a summer moth lies beneath your own finger. He is the God whom you are grieving every day. Does it not make you tremble to think that your eternal destiny now hangs upon the will of Him whom you have angered and enraged? Doesn't this frighten and alarm you? If it does, I rejoice, because this may be the first effect of the Spirit's drawing of your soul. Oh, tremble to think that the God whom you have angered is the God upon whom your salvation or your condemnation entirely depends! Tremble, and *kiss the Son lest he be angry, and ye perish from the way when his wrath is kindled in a little while* (Psalm 2:12).

Chapter 8

The Gospel Feast

The plan of salvation is simply declared: *Believe on the Lord Jesus Christ, and thou shalt be saved* (Acts 16:31). For you who have violated all the precepts of God and have scorned His mercy and provoked His vengeance, there is still mercy proclaimed, because *whosoever shall call upon the name of the Lord shall be saved* (Romans 10:13). *This is a faithful saying and worthy of acceptation by all, that Christ Jesus came into the world to save sinners, of whom I am first* (1 Timothy 1:15). *All that the Father gives me shall come to me, and he that comes to me I will in no wise cast out* (John 6:37), for *he is able also to save to the uttermost those that come unto God by him, seeing he ever lives to make intercession for them* (Hebrews 7:25).

All that God asks of you is that you will simply look at His bleeding, dying Son and trust your souls in the hands of Him whose name alone can save from death and hell. Is it not a remarkable thing that the proclamation

of this gospel does not receive the unanimous accep-
tance of all? One would think that as soon as it was
preached *that whosoever believes in him should not perish
but have eternal life* (John 3:15), everyone would cast
away his sins and iniquities, lay hold of Jesus Christ,
and look to His cross alone. But such is the desperate
evil of our nature and the destructive depravity of our
character that this message is despised, the invitation
to the gospel feast is rejected,
and there are many who are
enemies of God by wicked
works. They are enemies to
the God who preaches Christ.
They are enemies to Him who sent His Son to give His
life a ransom for many. It is strange that it should be
this way, yet nevertheless it is a fact. This is why there
is the need for the command to *compel them to come
in* (Luke 14:23).

Come and be welcomed
at the marriage
feast of His love.

You might not be wealthy, but this is no barrier to
the kingdom of heaven, because God has not exempted
from His grace those who have little food and who do
not have nice clothes. In fact, if there is any distinction made, the distinction is on your side and for your
benefit: *unto you is this word of saving health sent* (Acts
13:26). And *the poor have the gospel preached to them*
(Matthew 11:5). You have no faith, no integrity, no
good works, no grace, and worst of all, you have no
hope. Come and be welcomed at the marriage feast of
His love. *Whosoever will, let him take of the water of
life freely* (Revelation 22:17).

You are not only poor, but you are impaired. There

was a time when you thought you could work out your own salvation without God's help, when you could perform good works, attend to ceremonies, and get to heaven by yourselves, but now you are incapacitated. The sword of the law has cut off your hands, and you can no longer work. You say with bitter sorrow:

> "The best performance of my hands,
>> Dares not appear before Thy throne."[3]

You have lost all power to obey the law. You feel that even when you want to do good, evil is present with you (Romans 7:21). You are wounded. You have given up, as an abandoned hope, all attempts to save yourself, because you are incapacitated and your arms are gone. But you are worse off than that, for if you could not work your way to heaven, you could still walk your way there along the road by faith; but you are maimed in the feet as well as in the hands. You feel that you cannot believe, that you cannot repent, that you cannot obey the conditions of the gospel. You feel that you are utterly powerless in every respect to do anything that can be pleasing to God. I stand before you to lift up the blood-stained banner of the cross: *Whosoever shall call upon the name of the Lord shall be saved*; and to you I cry, *Whosoever will, let him take of the water of life freely.*

There is yet another class. You are double-minded. You are swaying between two opinions. Sometimes you are seriously inclined, and at another time worldly

---

3   From Isaac Watts' hymn "I Boast No More."

pleasures call you away. What little progress you do make in Christianity is weak. You have a little strength, but it is so little that you only make painful progress. The word of this salvation is sent to you, also. Even though you waver between two opinions, the Master sends you this message: *How long shall ye halt between two opinions? If the LORD is God, follow him; but if Baal, then follow him* (1 Kings 18:21). *Consider your ways* (Haggai 1:7). *Set thine house in order, for thou shalt die and not live* (Isaiah 38:1). Because I will do this, *prepare to meet thy God, O Israel* (Amos 4:12). Hesitate no longer, but make the decision to side with God and His truth.

There is another group of people – the blind. You cannot see yourselves, you think yourselves good when you are full of evil, and you exchange bitter for sweet and sweet for bitter, darkness for light and light for darkness. *Woe unto those that call evil good and good evil; that put darkness for light and light for darkness; that put bitter for sweet and sweet for bitter!* (Isaiah 5:20). You blind souls who cannot see your lost condition, who do not believe that sin is really as sinful as it is, and who will not be persuaded to think that God is a just and righteous God, to you I am sent. To you, too, who cannot see the Savior, who see no beauty in Him that you should desire Him (Isaiah 53:2), who see no excellence in virtue, no joy in Christianity, no happiness in serving God, no delight in being His children, to you, also, I speak.

Go out into the highways and hedges and compel them to come in that my house may be filled (Luke 14:23).

Here we bring in all classes and conditions of people: the businessman upon his horse in the highway, the woman trudging about her business, and the thief robbing the unsuspecting traveler. All of these are in the highway, and they are all to be compelled to come in. There, away in the hedges, lie some poor souls whose refuges of lies are swept away and who seek to find some little shelter for their weary heads. This is the universal command – *compel them to come in.*

Philip Melanchthon said it well: "Old Adam is too strong for young Melanchthon." It would be as futile for a little child to try to force Sampson to do something against his will as it would be for me to try to lead a sinner to the cross of Christ in the flesh. I see the great mountain of human depravity and dull indifference, but by faith I cry, *Who art thou, O great mountain before Zerubbabel? Thou shalt be reduced to a plain* (Zechariah 4:7).

Unconverted, unreconciled, unregenerate men and women, I must compel you to come in! Permit me, first of all, to confront you in the highways of sin and again tell you my duty. The king of heaven sends a gracious invitation to you. He says, *For I do not desire the death of him that dies, said the Lord GOD; therefore turn yourselves, and ye shall live* (Ezekiel 18:32). *Then come, shall the LORD say, and we shall be even; if your sins were as scarlet, they shall be made as white as snow; if they were red like crimson, they shall become as wool* (Isaiah 1:18). Let me tell you what the king has done for you. He knew your guilt, and He foresaw that you would ruin yourself. He knew that His justice would demand your blood, and in order to escape this difficulty and that His justice might have what it required that you might still be saved, *Jesus Christ died.*

Will you glance at this picture for just a moment? You see a man on His knees in the garden of Gethsemane sweating drops of blood. Next, you see that sorrowful sufferer tied to a pillar and lashed with terrible scourges until His shoulder bones are seen like white islands in the midst of a sea of blood. Then, you see the same man hanging on the cross with hands extended and His feet nailed firm, dying, groaning, bleeding. You hear Him say, *It is finished* (John 19:30). Jesus Christ of Nazareth has done all of this in order that God might consistently, with His justice, pardon sin. The message to you is this: *Believe on the Lord Jesus Christ, and thou shalt be saved* (Acts 16:31). That is, trust Him, renounce your works and your ways, and set your heart on this man alone, who gave Himself for sinners.

Do you turn away? You tell me it means nothing to you, that you cannot listen to it now, but you will listen to me some other time. You must go your way now and tend to your farm and merchandise. Stop! I was not told to merely tell you and then go about my business. No. I am told to compel you to come in. Permit me to say – and to this God is my witness – that I am deeply sincere in my desire that you would comply with this command of God.

Do you ignore it? Do you still refuse it? Then I must change my tone for a minute. I will not just tell you the message and invite you as I do with all sincerity; I will go further. Sinner, in God's name, I command you to repent and believe. Do you ask me where I get my authority? I am an ambassador of heaven. I command you to believe in the Lord Jesus Christ, not on my own authority, but on the authority of Him who said, *Go ye into all the world and preach the gospel to every creature. He that believes and is baptized shall be saved, but he that believes not shall be condemned* (Mark 16:15-16).

Do you turn away and say you will not listen to the authority of God? Then I will change my tone again. Let me tell you from my own soul what I know of Him. I, too, once despised Him. He knocked at the door of my heart, and I refused to open it. He came to me, times without number, morning by morning and night by night. He examined my conscience and spoke to me by His Spirit. When at last the thunders of the law prevailed in my conscience, I thought that Christ was cruel and unkind. Oh, I can never forgive myself that I thought so badly of Him; but what a loving reception I had when I went to Him. I thought He would strike me down, but His hand was not clenched in anger, but was opened wide in mercy. I fully thought that His eyes would dart lightning flashes of wrath upon me. Instead, they were full of tears. He fell upon my neck and kissed me. He took off my rags, clothed me with His righteousness, and caused my soul to sing aloud for joy, while in the house of my heart and in the house of His church there was music

> Do you ask me where I get my authority? I am an ambassador of heaven.

and dancing, because His son whom He had lost was found, and he who was dead was made alive.

I exhort you, then, to look to Jesus Christ and to be made glad. Sinner, you will never regret it. You will have no desire to go back to your state of condemnation. You will go out of Egypt and into the Promised Land, and you will find it flowing with milk and honey. You will find the trials of Christian life heavy, but grace will make them light. As for the joys and delights of being a child of God, if I lie, you will accuse me with it in days to come. If you will *taste and see that the Lord is good* (Psalm 34:8), I believe that you will find that He is not only good, but better than human lips could ever describe.

I do not know what arguments to use with you. I appeal to your own self-interests. Would it not be better for you to be reconciled to the God of heaven than to be His enemy? What are you gaining by opposing God? Are you happier because you are His enemy? Answer, pleasure seeker. Have you found delights in that cup? Answer me, self-righteous man. Have you found rest for the sole of your foot in all your works? Oh, you who go about to establish your own righteousness, I ask you to let your conscience speak. Have you found it to be a happy path? Ah, my friend, *Why do ye spend money for that which is not bread? and your labour for that which does not satisfy? Hearken diligently unto me, and eat ye that which is good, and let your soul delight itself in fatness* (Isaiah 55:2).

I exhort you by everything that is sacred and solemn, by everything that is important and eternal, flee for your lives, do not look behind you, do not stay in all the plain (see Genesis 19:17), do not stay until you have proved and found a share in the blood of Jesus Christ, that blood which cleanses us from all sin (1 John 1:7). Are you still cold and indifferent? Will the blind man refuse to allow me to lead him to the feast? Will not the weak man refuse to allow me to walk side-by-side with him? Must I use some stronger words? Must I use some other compulsion to compel you to come in?

From the grey-headed elderly person down to the child of tender age, if you do not lay hold on Christ, your blood will be on your own head. If there is power in man to bring his fellow man (as there is when we are helped by the Holy Spirit), that power will be exercised. I urge you to stop and consider. Do you know who it is you are rejecting? You are rejecting Christ, your only Savior. *For no one can lay another foundation than that laid, which is Jesus the Christ* (1 Corinthians 3:11). *Neither is there salvation in any other, for there is no other name under heaven given among men in which we can be saved* (Acts 4:12).

I cannot bear that you would reject Jesus, because I know what you are missing. The day is coming when you will want a Savior. It will not be long before the weary months will have ended and your strength begins to decline. Your pulse will fail you, your strength will depart, and you and the grim monster, death, must face each other. What will you do in the swelling of Jordan without a Savior? Deathbeds are fearful things without the Lord Jesus Christ. It is a fearful thing to die in any way. Even he who has the best hope and the most triumphant faith finds that death is not something to laugh at.

It can be a fearful and intimidating thing to pass from the seen to the unseen, from the mortal to the immortal, from time to eternity, and you will find it hard to go through the iron gates of death without the sweet wings of angels to carry you to the portals of the skies. It will be a difficult thing to die without Christ. I cannot help thinking of you. I can imagine you near death, and I picture myself standing at your bedside, hearing your cries, knowing you are dying without hope. I cannot bear the thought that I am standing by your coffin now, looking into your clay-cold face and saying, "This man despised Christ and neglected the great salvation." I think about what bitter tears I will weep if I think that I have neglected to do all that I could to help you, and how those eyes closed in death will seem to blame me and say, "You were not serious with me. You amused me and preached to me, but you did not plead with me. You did not know what Paul meant when he said, *Now then we are ambassadors for Christ, as though God did exhort you by us; we beseech you in Christ's name, be ye reconciled to God"* (2 Corinthians 5:20).

I picture myself standing at the throne of God. As the Lord lives, the day of judgment is coming. Do you believe that? You are not an infidel, so your conscience will not permit you to doubt the Scripture. Perhaps you may have pretended to do so, but you cannot. You feel there must be a day when God will judge the world in righteousness. I can picture you standing in the midst of that crowd, and the eye of God is focused on you. It seems to you that He is not looking anywhere else, but only at you. He summons you before Him, reads your sins, and says, *Depart from me, ye cursed, into eternal fire, prepared for the devil and his angels* (Matthew 25:41). I cannot bear to think of you in that position. It seems like every hair on my head will stand on end to think of anyone being damned.

Since I must stand before my Judge in the end, I feel that I will not make full proof of my ministry unless I beg with many tears that you would be saved, that you would look to Jesus Christ and receive His glorious salvation. Does this not help? Are all our pleadings lost upon you? Do you turn a deaf ear?

Then again, I change my tone. Sinner, I have pleaded with you as a man pleads with his friend. If it was for my own life, I could not speak more passionately than I speak concerning yours. Therefore, if you ignore these pleas, I have something else – I must warn you of what is to come. You will not always have such warnings as these. A day is coming when the voice of every gospel minister will be hushed, at least for you, because your ear will be cold in death. There will be no more threatening. Instead, it will be the fulfilment of the threatening. There will be no promise, no proclamations of pardon and of mercy, and no blood that brings peace. Instead, you will be in the land where the preaching of the gospel is forbidden, because it would be futile.

I instruct you, then, to listen to this voice that now addresses your conscience. If not, God will speak to you in His wrath and say to you in His fiery displeasure, *Because I have called and ye refused; I have stretched out my hand, and no one responded; for because ye have disregarded all my counsel and rejected my reproof: I also will laugh at your calamity; I will mock when your fear comes upon you* (Proverbs 1:24-26).

Sinner, I warn you again. It is only a short time before you may have to hear these warnings. Come, let the promise of judgment influence you. I do not threaten to alarm you without cause, but I hope that telling you what will surely happen may drive you to the place where God has prepared the feast of the gospel. Have I exhausted all that I can say? No, I will come to you again. Tell me what it is that keeps you from Christ.

I hear someone say, "It is because I feel that I'm too guilty."

That cannot be, my friend; that cannot be.

"But, sir, I am the chief of sinners."

Friend, you are not. The chief of sinners died and went to heaven many years ago. His name was Saul of Tarsus, afterwards called Paul the apostle. He was the chief of sinners. I know he spoke the truth.

"No," you still say, "I am too vile."

You cannot be worse than the *chief* of sinners. You must be at least second worst. Even supposing you are the worst now alive, you are second worst, because he was chief. But suppose you are the worst; isn't that the very reason you should come to Christ? The worse a person is, the more reason he should go to the hospital or physician. The poorer you are, the more reason you should accept the charity of another. Christ does not want any merits of yours. He gives freely. The worse you are, the more welcome you are.

Let me ask you a question. Do you think you will ever get better by stopping your sinful ways while you are apart from Christ? If so, you still know very little about the way of salvation. No, the longer you stay away, the worse you will grow. Your hope will grow weaker. Your despair will become stronger. The nail with which Satan has fastened you down will be more firmly clenched, and you will be less hopeful than ever. Come, I urge you. There is nothing to be gained by delay, but by delay everything may be lost.

"But," cries another, "I feel that I cannot believe."

My friend, you never will believe if you look first at your believing. Remember, I don't invite you to faith, but I invite you to Christ.

You ask, "What is the difference?"

Just this. If you first of all say, "I want to believe a certain thing," you never do it. Your first inquiry must be, "What is this thing that I am to believe?" Faith will come as the consequence of that search. Our first business doesn't have to do with faith, but with Christ. Come, I beg you, to Calvary's mount and see the cross. Behold the Son of God, He who made the heavens and the earth, dying for your sins. Look to Him. Is there not power in Him to save? Look at His face so full of compassion. Is there not love in His heart to prove that He is willing to save? O sinner, the sight of Christ will help you to believe. Do not believe first and then go to

Christ, or your faith will be a worthless thing. Go to Christ without any faith, and cast yourself upon Him, sink or swim.

I hear another cry, "Sir, you do not know how often I have been invited and how long I have rejected the Lord." I do not know, and I do not want to know. All I know is that my Master has sent me to compel you to come in; so come along with me now. You may have rejected a thousand invitations; don't make this the thousandth-and-one. You have been up to the house of God, and you have only been gospel-hardened.

I cannot let you continue on in such empty excuses as that. If you have lived so many years disregarding Christ, there are so many reasons why you should not disregard Him now. Did I hear you whisper that this was not a convenient time? Then what must I say to you? When will that convenient time come? Will it come when you are in hell? Will that time be convenient? Will it come when you are on your deathbed? Will it come then? Or when the burning sweat is scalding your brow, or when the cold clammy sweat is there – will those be convenient times? Will it be a convenient time when you are filled with pain and you are on the borders of the tomb?

I have no authority to ask you to come to Christ tomorrow. The invitation is, *Today if ye will hear his voice, harden not your hearts, as in the provocation* (Hebrews 3:15), for the Spirit says *Then come, shall the LORD say, and we shall be even; if your sins were as scarlet, they shall be made as white as snow; if they were red like crimson, they shall become as wool* (Isaiah 1:18). Why would you put it off?

It may be the last warning you will ever have. You may never again have such an earnest discourse addressed to you. You may not be pleaded with as I plead with you now. You may go away, and God may say, He *is given over to idols; leave him* (Hosea 4:17). He will throw the reins upon your neck, and then your course will be certain, but it will be certain damnation and swift destruction.

Is it all in vain? Will you not come to Christ now? Then what more can I do? I have only one more thing I can try, and I will try that. I am permitted to weep for you. I can pray for you. You can scorn my attempts if you like. You can laugh at the preacher and call him overzealous if you desire. He will not rebuke you. He will not bring an accusation against you to the great Judge. Your offence, as far as he is concerned, is forgiven before it is committed; but remember that the message you are rejecting is a message from One who loves you, and it is given to you by the voice of another who loves you. You may play your soul away with the devil, and you may think that this is a matter of no importance, but there is at least one who is serious about your soul. I'll say again that when words fail us, we can give tears, because words and tears are the arms with which gospel ministers compel people to come in.

I heard just the other day about a young man whose father's hope was that he would be brought to Christ.

> It may be the last warning you will ever have.

He became acquainted, however, with an unbeliever, and now he neglects his business and lives in a daily course of sin. I saw his father's poor pale face. I did not ask him to tell me the story himself, because I felt like it would bring up sorrow and open a wound. I fear, sometimes, that a good man's gray hairs may be brought with sorrow to the grave.

Young men, you do not pray for yourselves, but your mothers wrestle in prayer for you. You will not think of your own souls, but your father's anxiety is exercised for you. I have been at prayer meetings where I have heard children of God pray there, and they could not have prayed with more earnestness and more intensity of anguish for their lost children than if they had been seeking their own soul's salvation. Is it not strange that we would be ready to move heaven and earth for your salvation, and yet you still have no thought for your own soul and no regard for eternal things?

Chapter 9

Warnings to Certain Sinners

Cain was of the wicked one and slew his brother (Genesis 4). *The way of Cain* (Jude 11) is not hard to describe. Cain is too proud to offer atonement for his sin; he prefers his own way of sacrifice. He presents a bloodless offering. He hates the obedience of faith. He murders the faithful Abel.

Observe the way of Cain, and beware, you proud, self-righteous ones, so that you do not follow the same way, for the steps are few from self-righteous pride to hatred of true believers, and murder is not far beyond that. The seed of every wicked act can be found in the proud spirit of self-justification, and it is a great mercy that it does not show itself in all its terrific ripeness more often. You who boast of your own merits, see the mangled body of the first martyr, for that is the full-blown development of your rebellious self-conceit. Lord, deliver us from all pride and boasting, all self-righteousness, and all hatred of the cross of Christ.

There are many people whose brother's blood cries to God from the ground (see Genesis 4:10).

There is the seducer. He spoke with flattering words and talked of love, but the poison of asps was under his tongue, for lust was in his heart. He came to a beautiful temple as a worshipper, but he committed infamous sacrilege, and left that to be the haunt of demons which once was the palace of purity.

Such men are received into society and are looked upon as gentlemen, while the fallen woman, the harlot, can only hide herself beneath the shadow of night. No one will make excuse for her sin, but the man, the criminal, is called a respectable and reputable man. He can fill places of trust and positions of honor, and there are none who point the finger of scorn at him. Sir, the voice of that poor fallen sister's blood cries to heaven against you, and in the day of judgment her damnation shall be on you. All the shame into which you have plunged her will lie at your door. Among the dreadful sights of hell, two eyes will glare at you through the murky darkness like the eyes of serpents, burning their way into your inmost soul. "You deceived me and lured me to the pit," she says. "Your arms dragged me down to hell, and here I lie to curse you forever and ever as the author of my eternal ruin."

There is one sinner who can look upon this in a serious light. Who is it who has gone down to the pit? You over there, who is it who died just a few days ago? The woman who loved you as she loved her own soul, who idolized you and thought you were an angel. Shall I say it before God and to your face? You ruined her! And what next, sir? You cast her off as though she were only dirt, and you threw her into the gutter with a broken heart. Once she was there, she fell into despair, because her god cast her off, for you were her god. Her despair led to dreadful consequences and to deeper ruin still.

She has gone, and you are glad about it, because you think you will hear no more of her. Sir, you *will* hear of it! As long as you live, her spirit will haunt you. It will follow you to the filthy joy which you have planned for your future. On your deathbed she will be there to twist her fingers in your hair, to tear your soul out of your body and drag it down to the hell appointed for such evil people as you. You spilled her blood, the blood of her who trusted you – a fair, frail thing, worthy to be an angel's sister – and you pulled her down and made her a devil's tool! God save you! If He does not, your damnation will be sevenfold. Oh, you son of the devil, what will your doom be when God deals with you as you deserve? Are these scorching words? Not half as scorching as I would like to make them. I would send them hissing into your soul if I were able, not so much to condemn you, but with the hope that though you cannot make good the trouble you have done, you can still turn from the error of your ways to seek the Savior's blood and find pardon for this great iniquity.

Then there are those who educate youth in sin. These are Satan's captains and marshals. They are strong men with corrupt hearts, who are never more pleased than when they see the buds of evil swelling and ripening into crime. We have known some such men who possess an evil eye, who not only loved sin themselves, but delighted in it in others. They patted the boy on his back when he uttered his first profanity, and rewarded him when he committed his first theft.

Satan has his Sunday-school teachers. Hell has its missionaries who travel sea and land to make one convert and make him ten times more a child of hell than they are themselves. Most of our villages are cursed with one such wretch, and is there even a single street in any big city on which one or more such fiends do not live? Wretch, have you sought to entangle them in your net? Have you, like the spider, thrown first one strand of web around them and then another, until you have them safely in your coils to drag them down to the den of Beelzebub? If so, then the voice of your brother's blood cries from the ground. At the judgment, this will be a witness that you will not be able to disprove – the witness of the blood of souls ruined by your sinful and evil training. Beware, you who hunt for the precious life!

Then there are some corrupt people who, if they see young converts, take pride in putting stumbling blocks in their way. As soon as they discover that there is a little working of conscience in someone, they laugh, sneer, and point their finger. How often I have seen this in a husband who tries to prevent his wife's attendance at a prayer meeting, or in the young man who ridicules his friend because he felt the power of God's Holy Spirit and begins to read the Scriptures, pray, and think about changing his ways! This happens too frequently in our great establishments in London, where one young man kneels to pray, and many laugh at him and insult him. They are not content to perish themselves. Like dogs pursuing a deer, so the wicked will hunt the godly.

You who are the enlisting sergeants for the evil Prince of Darkness, you who seem never as happy as when you set traps for souls to entice them to destruction, I solemnly warn you. Heed the warning, to prevent God's avenging angel overtaking you without warning with the sword that will strike your neck and cause you to feel how terrible a thing it is to have tried to ruin the servants of the living God.

Then there is the infidel. He is the person who is not content to keep his sin to himself, but feels the need to publish his wickedness. He climbs to the top of the platform and blasphemes the Almighty to his face, defies the Eternal, takes Scripture to make it the subject of unholy jokes, and makes Christianity a theme for comedy. If this is you, be careful, for there will be a tragedy in the future in which you will be the chief sufferer!

What should I say of those men who are far more diligent than half of God's ministers, whose names we see engraved on plaques on every wall? They will go from town to town, and never seem content unless they are preaching against something that is pure, and lovely, and of good report, or proclaiming things that would make your cheeks drain of their color if you heard them. They are dreadful things against the Most

High, such as David heard when he said, *Horror has taken hold upon me because of the wicked that forsake thy law* (Psalm 119:53).

I address such people, because the voice of your brother's blood cries out to God. The young men you have deluded, the working men you have led astray, the sinners whose lullaby you have sung, the souls you have poisoned with your foul drinks, the multitudes you have deceived – all these will stand up in the end, a huge army, and pointing their fingers at you, they will demand your swift destruction, because you lured them to their doom.

And what shall I say of the unfaithful preacher? He is the slumbering watchman of souls, the man who gave testimony at God's altar that he was called by the Holy Spirit to preach the Word of God. He is the man upon whose lips people's ears waited with attention while he stood like a priest at God's altar to teach Israel God's laws. He is the man who performed his duties half-asleep, in a dull and careless manner, until others also slept and thought Christianity was not to be taken very seriously.

What shall I say of the pastor with an unholy life, whose corrupt practice outside of the pulpit has made the most meaningful things from the pulpit to be powerless. He has blunted the edge of the sword of the Spirit and turned the back of God's army in the day of battle.

What should I say about the preacher who has amused his audience with fine-sounding words and humorous stories when he ought to have stirred their consciences. He has been more concerned about fancy sermon outlines than of proclaiming the judgment of God. He has preached a dead morality when he ought to have lifted Christ on high as Moses lifted the serpent in the wilderness.

What should I say about those who have dwindled away their congregations, who have sown strife and division in churches of Christ that were once happy, peaceful, and prosperous? What should I say about the men who have joked from the pulpit about the most serious things, whose lives have been so devoid of holy passion and devout enthusiasm that people have thought truth to be a lie, Christianity a performance, prayer powerless, the Spirit of God a delusion, and eternity a joke? Among all who will need eternal compassion, surely the unfaithful, unholy, passionless minister of Christ will be the most to be pitied! What did I say? No, rather he is the most contemptible, the most despicable, and the most accursed! Surely, every thunderbolt will make his brow its target, and every arrow of God will seek his conscience as its mark.

> If I must perish, let me suffer any way but as a minister who has desecrated the pulpit.

If I must perish, let me suffer any way but as a minister who has desecrated the pulpit by a slumbering style of ministry, by a lack of passion for souls. How will such men answer for it at the throne of God – the smooth things, the polite and agreeable words, the whitewashing of men with the watered-down paint of peace, when they should have dealt with them honestly as in God's name? Sirs, if we never play the part of the Sons of Thunder, we will hear God's thunders in our ears forever and ever, and we will be cursed of men and cursed of the Most High without end. In hell we will have this lament peculiar to ourselves: "We preached what we did not feel. We testified of what we did not know. People did not receive our witness, for we were hypocrites and deceivers, and now we go down, richly deserving it, to the very lowest depths of eternal punishment."

But the voice of your brother's blood cries to God from the ground, even though you are not an infidel lecturer, even though you have not been degenerate, even though you never taught heresy, and even though you have spread no schism. If your life is unholy, your brother's blood is on your own head.

"Oh," says one, "If I sin, I sin to myself."

Impossible!

The deadly contagious illness might say, "I am deadly to myself alone." Cholera might say, "My deadly breath is for myself only." Your example spreads. You, like the leper, leave uncleanliness on everything you touch. The very atmosphere which surrounds you breeds disease. What others see you do, they learn to do. Some may even rival you and exceed you, but if you taught them their lessons and they learn to read in hell's book better than you, all that they learn afterwards will come to your door, because they learned the elements of sin from your practice.

I am afraid many people never look at their transgressions in this light. You cannot help being leaders and teachers. If in your own house you are a drunkard, your boys will be drunkards too! I have heard of a man who flogged his son for swearing, swearing at him the whole time he did it. We know instances of people who feel as if they would sooner bury their children than see them grow up like themselves, but how can it be helped?

Your practice must and will influence your children, and not only your children, but all with whom you come into contact in the world. Do not think, if you are an employer, that your employees can know how you live your life without being affected by that knowledge. There may be some among them who have an inward principle that will not yield to temptation, but I know of hardly anything more dangerous than for a number of people to constantly come into contact with one whom they look up to as a teacher who is also a teacher of the arts of sin and a leader of damnation to their souls. Be careful; if not for yourselves, then for others, or the voice of your brother's blood will cry unto God from the ground.

What should the cry be against open sinners and unbelievers? It would be an awful thing to pray for a man's damnation, but there are some people I know of who do so much harm while they live, that if they were dead, people would breathe more freely. I know a village where there lives a man who contaminates half the population. There is a malicious look upon his face that causes virtue to blush and a contemptuous smirk that causes courage to cower. He is a wretch, so well taught and so deeply instructed in the realm of iniquity, that wherever he goes he finds no one a match for him, either in his reasoning or in the infamous conclusions that he draws. He is a man who is a deadly upas tree, dropping black poison upon all beneath his shadow.[4]

I once thought that I would half pray that the man would die and go to his destruction, but one must not do that. Yet, if he were gone, the saints might say, "It is well." Just as the saints will say "Hallelujah!" over Babylon when it is destroyed and the smoke of her torment goes up forever (Revelation 19:3), I thought that same shout of "Hallelujah!" might be said when those people against whom the blood of many young people cries out to God from the ground go to their doom, for God has judged the great sinner who made the people of the earth drunk with the wine of his fornication (Revelation 18:3).

What can we do to be rid of the past? Can tears of repentance do it? No. Can promises of change make a blank page where there are so many blots and blemishes? No. Nothing we can do removes our sin. But can't the future make up for the past? Cannot future zeal wipe out past carelessness? Cannot the endeavor of our life yet to come make amends for the idleness or vice of the life that is past? No. The blood of our brothers has been shed, and we cannot gather it up. The harm we have caused cannot be undone!

Souls that are lost through us cannot now be saved. The gates of hell are so shut that they can never be opened. There is no restitution we can make. The redemption of the soul is precious, and it ceases forever. The sin cannot be washed away by repentance or

4   The upas tree is a tropical Asian tree, the sap of which contains poisonous glycosides. The sap has been used for poison arrows. The tree was once thought to have given off a poisonous gas.

removed by reformation. What then? There would be hopeless despair for every one of us if there were not another blood – the blood of One called Jesus. It cries from the ground, too, and the voice of that blood says, *Father, forgive them. Father, forgive them* (Luke 23:34).

I hear a voice that says, "Vengeance, vengeance, vengeance," like the voice of Jonah in Nineveh, enough to make everyone clothe himself in sackcloth; but a sweeter and louder cry comes up, "Mercy, mercy, mercy." The Father bows His head and says, "Whose blood is that?" The voice replies, "It is the blood of your only begotten Son, shed on Calvary for sin."

> Hate the sin that is past and trust in Jesus for the future.

The Father lays His thunder aside, sheathes His sword, stretches out His hand, and cries to you sons and daughters of men, "Come unto Me, and I will have mercy upon you. Turn, turn from your ways. I will pour out My Spirit upon you and you shall live. Repent and believe the gospel." Hate the sin that is past and trust in Jesus for the future. He is able to completely save all who come to God by Him, for the blood of Jesus Christ, God's dear Son, cleanses us from all sin (1 John 1:7).

Flee, sinner, flee! The avenger of the blood that you have shed pursues you in haste. With feet that are winged and a heart that is thirsty for blood, he pursues you. Run, man, run! The city of refuge is before you. It is there along the narrow way of faith. Fly, fly, for unless you reach that city before he overtakes you, he will smite you, and one blow will be your everlasting ruin.

Do not linger! Do not stop and look at the field on the

left, for you will stain that field with your blood if you linger there! Do not stop at that tavern on the right. Stop for none of these things! He comes! Hear his footsteps on the hard highway! He comes, he comes, he comes now! Oh, that you may pass through the entrance of the refuge city! Trust the Son of God. Your sin will be forgiven, and you will have entered into everlasting life.

Chapter 10

Christ the Son of Man

How fond our Master was of the sweet title the "Son of Man"! If He had chosen, He might always have spoken of Himself as the Son of God, the Everlasting Father, the Wonderful, the Counselor, or the Prince of Peace. He has a thousand wonderful titles, as magnificent as the throne of heaven, but He does not care to use them. To express His humility and let us see the lowliness of Him whose yoke is easy and whose burden is light, He does not call himself the Son of God, but He speaks of Himself continually as the Son of Man who came down from heaven.

Let us learn a lesson in humility from our Savior. Never let us pursue great titles or proud degrees. After all, what are they but empty distinctions which allow one worm to be known from another? He who has the most is still a worm and his nature is no better than that of his colleagues. If Jesus called Himself the Son of Man when He had far greater names, let us learn to humble ourselves with others of low position, knowing that he who humbles himself will in due time be exalted.

I think, though, that there is a sweeter thought than this in the name *Son of Man*. It seems to me that Christ loved manhood so much that He always desired to honor it. Since it is a high honor, and indeed the greatest dignity of manhood that Jesus Christ was the Son of Man, He is inclined to display this name, so that He may, as it were, put a badge of honor upon the chest of manhood and put a crown upon its head.

Son of Man – whenever Jesus said that, He seemed to put a halo around the head of Adam's children. Yet there is perhaps a lovelier thought still. Jesus Christ called Himself the Son of Man because He loved to be one of us. It was a huge step down for Him to come from heaven and to be incarnate. It was a mighty act of condescension when He left the harps of angels and the songs of cherubim to mingle with the common herd of His own creatures. But even though it was condescension, He loved it. You will remember that when He became incarnate, He did not become so in the dark. When God brought forth the only begotten into the world, He said, "Let all the angels of God worship Him." It was proclaimed in heaven. It was not done as a dark secret that Jesus Christ would do in the night so that none would know about it. All the angels of God were brought to witness the arrival of a Savior as a tiny baby, sleeping upon a virgin's breast and lying in a manger.

Ever afterwards, and even now, He was never ashamed to confess that He was man. He never looked back upon His incarnation with the slightest regret, but always regarded it as a joyous remembrance that He had become the Son of Man. All hail, blessed Jesus! We know how much You love us. We understand the greatness of Your mercy toward Your chosen ones, inasmuch as You always use the sweet name which acknowledges that we are bone of Your bone and flesh of Your flesh, and that You are one of them, a brother and a close relation.

I will tell you the people Christ will save. He will save those who are lost to themselves. Just imagine a ship at sea passing through a storm. The ship leaks, and the captain tells the passengers he fears they are lost. If they are far away from the shore and have sprung a leak, they pump with all their might, as long as they have any strength remaining. They seek to keep down the devouring element, and they still think they are not quite lost as long as they have power to use the pumps.

He will save those who are lost to themselves.

Finally, they see the ship cannot be saved. They give it up for lost and leap into the lifeboats. The boats are floating for many days, full of people who have barely any food to eat. "They are lost," we say, "lost out at sea." But they do not think so. They still cherish a hope that perhaps some stray ship might pass that way and pick them up. There is a ship on the horizon, and they strain their eyes to look at her. They lift each other up and wave a flag. They tear their clothes to make something which will attract attention, but the ship passes away. Night comes and they are forgotten. In the end, the very last mouthful of food has been consumed, and their strength fails them. They lay down their oars in the boat and lay themselves down to die.

You can imagine then how well they understand the awful meaning of the word *lost*. As long as they had any strength left, they felt they were not lost. As long as they could see a sail, they felt there was still hope. While there was still a dry biscuit or a drop of water remaining, they did not give up all for lost. Now the biscuit is gone and the water is gone; the strength has departed, and the oar lies still. They lie down to die by each other's side, mere skeletons. They should have been dead days earlier if they had died when all enjoyment of life had ceased. Now they know what it is to be lost, and across the shoreless waters they seem to hear their death-knell pealing forth that awful word: Lost! Lost! Lost!

In a spiritual sense, these are the people Christ came to save. Sinner, you too are condemned. Our father Adam steered the ship off course, she split upon a rock, and she is filling even to her deck now. No matter how hard you may pump your own morals and philosophy, you can never keep the waters of her depravity low enough to prevent the ship from sinking. We see that human nature is lost; it has gotten into the boat. She is a fair boat called the boat of Good Attempts. In her, you are striving to row with all your might to reach the shore, but your strength fails you.

You say, "I cannot keep God's law. The more I strive to keep it, the more I find it to be impossible for me to do so. I climb, but the higher I climb, the higher the top seems to be above me. When I was in the plains, I thought the mountain was only a moderate hill. Now I seem to have ascended halfway up its slope. There it is, higher than the clouds, and I cannot see the summit."

However, you gather up your strength and you try again. You row once more, and in the end, you are unable to do anything. So you lay down your oars and realize that if you are saved, it cannot be by your own works. Still, you have a little hope left. There are a few small pieces of dry biscuit remaining. You have heard that by participating in certain ceremonies you might be saved, and you chew your dry biscuit. Ultimately, that fails you, and you find that neither baptism, the Lord's supper, nor any other outward rite can make you clean, for the leprosy lies deep within.

Knowing this, you still look out on the horizon. You still hope that there might be a sail coming, and while floating upon that deep of despair, you think you detect in the distance some new dogma or some fresh doctrine that may comfort you. It passes, however, like the wild phantom ship. It is gone, and you are left with the burning sky of God's vengeance above you and the deep waters of a bottomless hell beneath you. With fire in your heart and emptiness in that ship that was once so full of hope, you lie down in despair and cry, "Lord save me, or I perish!"

Is that your condition, my friend, or has that ever been your condition? If so, Christ came into the world to seek and to save you, and you He will save, and no one else. He will only save those who can claim for their title, "Lost," those who have understood in their own souls what it is to be lost in regard to all self-trust, all self-reliance, and all self-hope.

I can look back to the time when I knew that I was lost. I thought that God intended to destroy me. I imagined that because I felt myself to be lost, I was the special victim of Almighty vengeance. I even said to the Lord, "Have You set me as the target of all Your arrows? *Am I a sea, or a dragon, that thou settest a watch over me?* (Job 7:12). Have You sewed up my iniquities in a bag and sealed my transgressions with a seal? (Job 14:17). Will You never be gracious? Have You made me to be the center of all sorrow, and the chosen one of heaven to be cursed forever?" I was a fool! I didn't know then that those who have the curse in themselves are those whom God will bless – that we have the sentence of death in ourselves, that we should not trust in ourselves, but in Him who died for us and rose again.

Can you say that you are lost? Was there a time when you traveled with the caravan through this wild wilderness world? Have you left the caravan with your companions to find yourself in the midst of a sea of sand – a hopeless arid waste? Do you look around you and see no helper, and do you cast your eyes around and see no trust? Is the vulture circling in the sky, screaming with delight, because he hopes to soon feed upon your flesh and bones? Is the water bottle dry and does the bread fail you? Have you consumed the last of your dry dates and drunk the last of that unpleasant water from the bottle? Are you now without hope, without trust in yourself, and ready to lie down in despair?

Listen! The Lord your God loves you. Jesus Christ

has bought you with His blood. You are, and you shall be His. He has been seeking you all this time, and He has found you at last, in the vast howling wilderness. Now He will take you upon His shoulders and carry you to His house rejoicing, and the angels will be glad over your salvation.

Such people must and will be saved, and this is the description of those whom Jesus Christ came to save. Those He came to save, He will save. You – you lost ones who have lost all hope and self-confidence – will be saved. Even though death and hell would stand in the way, Christ will fulfill His promise and accomplish His plan.

For the most part, though, Christ finds His people in His own house. He finds them often in the worst of tempers and in the most hardened conditions. He softens their hearts, awakens their consciences, subdues their pride, and takes them to Himself; but they would never come to Him unless He went to them. Sheep go astray, but they do not come back again of themselves. Ask the shepherd whether his sheep come back, and he will tell you, "No, sir. They will wander, but they never return." If you ever find a sheep that came back on its own, then you may hope to find a sinner who will come to Christ on his own. No; it must be sovereign grace that seeks the sinner and brings him home.

When Christ seeks them, He saves them. Having caught him at last, like the ram of old, in the thorns of conviction, He does not take a knife and slay him

> When Christ seeks them, He saves them.

as the sinner expects, but He takes him by the hand of mercy and begins to comfort and save. The Christ who seeks you today and who has sought you for a long time by His providence will save you. He will first find you when you are emptied of self, and then He will save you. When you are stripped, He will bring you the best robe and put it on you. When you are dying, He will breathe life into your nostrils. When you feel yourselves condemned, He will come and blot out your iniquities like a cloud, and your transgressions like a thick cloud (Isaiah 44:22). Do not fear, you hopeless and helpless souls, for Christ seeks you today, and He will save you. He will save you here, save you living, save you dying, save you in time, save you in eternity, and give you – even you, the lost ones – a portion among those who are sanctified.

Chapter 11

The Great Remedy

We can learn nothing of the gospel except by feeling its truths. No single truth of the gospel is ever truly known and really learned until we have tested and tried and proved it, and its power has been exercised upon us. I heard of a naturalist who thought himself to be exceedingly wise regarding the natural history of birds, yet he had learned all he knew in his office, and had never so much as seen a bird either flying through the air or sitting upon its perch. He was just a fool, although he thought himself to be exceedingly wise.

There are some men who, like him, think of themselves as great theologians. They might even claim to have a doctor's degree in divinity. Yet, if we got to the root of the matter and asked them whether they ever saw or felt any of these things of which they talked, they would have to say, "No. I know these things in the letter, but not in the spirit. I understand them as a matter of theory, but not as part of my own consciousness and experience."

Be assured that just as the naturalist who was merely the student of other people's observations knew nothing, so the person who pretends to be pious but has never entered into the depths and power of its doctrines or felt the influence of them upon his heart knows nothing, and all the knowledge he pretends to have is just disguised ignorance. There are some sciences that can possibly be learned by the head, but the science of Christ crucified can only be learned by the heart.

No one can know the magnitude of sin until he has felt it, because there is no measuring rod for sin except its condemnation in our own conscience when the law of God speaks to us with a terror that may be felt.

Some people imagine that the gospel was devised, in some way or other, to soften the harshness of God towards sin. How mistaken is that idea! There is no more harsh condemnation of sin anywhere than in the gospel.

The blood of Jesus Christ, his Son cleanses us from all sin (1 John 1:7). There lies the darkness; here stands the Lord Jesus Christ. What will He do with it? Will He go and speak to it and say, "This is no great evil. This darkness is just a little spot"? No. He looks at it and says, "This is terrible wickedness, darkness that may be felt. This is an exceeding great evil." Will He cover it up? Will He weave a mantle of excuse and wrap it around the iniquity? No. Whatever covering there may have been, He lifts it off, and He declares that when the Spirit of Truth is come, He will convince the world of sin, lay the sinner's conscience bare, and probe the wound to the bottom. Then what will He do? He will do a far better thing than make an excuse or pretend in any way to speak lightly of it. He will cleanse it all away and remove it entirely by the power and meritorious virtue of His own blood.

Nor does the gospel in any way give us hope that the claims of the law will be in any way loosened. Some imagine that under the old dispensation God demanded great things of man – that He placed burdens upon them that were too heavy to carry. They think that Christ came into the world to put a lighter law upon the shoulders of men, something that would be easier for them to obey, a law that they can more easily keep, or that if they break, would not result in such terrible punishment.

> The gospel did not come into the world to soften down the law.

This is not so. The gospel did not come into the world to soften down the law. *For verily I say unto you, Until heaven and earth pass away, not one jot or one tittle shall pass from the law until all is fulfilled* (Matthew 5:18). What God has said to the sinner in the law, He says to the sinner in the gospel. If He declares, *The soul that sins, it shall die* (Ezekiel 18:20), the testimony of the gospel is not contrary to the testimony of the law. If He declares that whoever breaks the sacred law will certainly be punished, the gospel also demands blood for blood, eye for eye, and tooth for tooth, and does not relax a solitary jot or tittle of its demands, but is as severe and as intensely just as the law itself.

Do you reply that Christ has certainly softened down the law? I reply, then, that you don't know the mission of Christ. That is no softening of the law. It is, as it were, the grinding of the edge of the dreadful sword of divine justice to make it far sharper than it seemed before. Christ has not put out the furnace; rather He seemed to heat it seven times hotter. Before Christ came, sin did not seem to be a big deal to me, but when He came, sin became exceedingly sinful to me, and all its dreaded ugliness became clear in the light.

Someone might say, "Surely the gospel, in some degree, removes the enormity of our sin. Doesn't it soften the punishment of sin?" No. Ezekiel says, *The soul that sins, it shall die*, and his sermon is alarming and dreadful. He sits down. Now comes Jesus Christ, the man of a loving countenance. What does He say regarding the punishment of sin? Our Lord Jesus Christ was all love, but He was all honesty, too. *Never has anyone spoken like this man*, it was said of Jesus when He spoke of the punishment of the lost (John 7:46). No other prophet but Jesus was the author of such fearful expressions as these:

> *He will burn up the chaff with fire that shall never be quenched.* (Matthew 3:12)

> *And they shall go away into eternal punishment.* (Matthew 25:46)

*Where their worm does not die, and the fire
is never quenched.* (Mark 9:44)

Stand at the feet of Jesus when He tells you about the
punishment of sin and the effect of iniquity, and you
will have far more reason to tremble there than you
would have done if Moses had been the preacher and
if Sinai had been in the background to conclude the
sermon. No, the gospel of Christ in no sense whatsoever
helps to make sin less. The proclamation of Christ is
the same as the utterance of Ezekiel of old: *The iniquity of the house of Israel and Judah is exceeding great*
(Ezekiel 9:9).

Our sins are immense. Every sin is significant, but
there are some that in our comprehension seem to be
more substantial than others. There are crimes that
an ordinary person could not mention. I could go to
great lengths in describing the degradation of human
nature in the sins that it has invented. It is amazing
how the ingenuity of man seems to have exhausted
itself in inventing fresh crimes. Surely there is not the
possibility of the invention of a new sin, but if there is,
man will invent it before long, for man seems to grow
in his deceptiveness and is full of wisdom in the dis-
covery of ways to destroy himself and in his attempts
to offend his Maker.

There are some sins that show an evil extent of
degraded thinking – some sins of which it is shameful
to speak and disgraceful to think. But *the blood of Jesus
Christ, his Son cleanses us from all sin* (1 John 1:7). There
may be some sins of which we cannot speak, but there

is no sin that the blood of Christ cannot wash away. Blasphemy, however profane; lust, however depraved; covetousness, however far it may have gone into theft and robbery; breach of the commandments of God, to whatever extent it may have run – all these may be pardoned and washed away through the blood of Jesus Christ. In all the long list of human sins, though that is as long as time, there stands only one sin that is unpardonable. No sinner has committed that one sin if he feels within himself a longing for mercy, because once that sin is committed, the soul becomes hardened, dead, and insensitive, and never afterward desires to find peace with God.

Therefore I declare to you, trembling sinner, that however serious your iniquity may be, whatever sin you may have committed, however far you may have exceeded all your fellow creatures, though you may have surpassed the Pauls and Magdalenes and all of the most wicked offenders in the wicked race of sin – the blood of Christ is still able to wash your sin away. I do not speak lightly of your sin, for it is exceedingly serious, but I speak more highly of the blood of Christ. As considerable as your sins are, the blood of Christ is greater still. Your sins are like great mountains, but the blood of Christ is like Noah's flood. Upward this blood will prevail, and the top of the mountains of your sin will be covered.

Whatever I may not be, one thing I know I am – a sinner, guilty, consciously guilty, and often miserable on account of that guilt. The Scripture says, *This is a faithful saying and worthy of acceptation by all, that*

Christ Jesus came into the world to save sinners (1 Timothy 1:15).

> "And when thine eye of faith is dim,
>   Still trust in Jesus, sink or swim;
> Thus, at His footstool, bow the knee,
>   And Israel's God thy peace shall be."[5]

Let me put my entire trust in the bloody sacrifice which He offered on my behalf. I will not depend upon my prayers, my good deeds, my feelings, my tears, my sermons, my thinking, my Bible reading, nor any of that. I will desire to have good works, but I will not put a shadow of trust in my good works.

> "Nothing in my hand I bring,
>   Simply to Thy cross I cling."[6]

If there is any power in Christ to save, I am saved. If there is an everlasting arm extended by Christ, and if that Savior who hung there was *God over all things, blessed for all the ages* (Romans 9:5), and if His blood is still displayed before the throne of God as the sacrifice for sin, then I cannot perish until the throne of God breaks and the pillars of God's justice crumble.

---

5   From "This Man Shall Be the Peace" by John Kent (1766-1843).
6   From "Rock of Ages" by Augustus M. Toplady (1740-1778).

Chapter 12

The Kiss of Reconciliation

The kiss is a token of enmity removed, of strife ended, and of peace established. You will remember that when Jacob met Esau, although the hearts of the brothers had been long estranged – fear had dwelt in the heart of one, and revenge had kindled its fires in the heart of the other – when they met, they were at peace with each other. They fell upon each other's neck and they kissed. It was the kiss of reconciliation.

The very first work of grace in the heart is for Christ to give the sinner the kiss of His affection and to prove His reconciliation to the sinner. In this same way, the father kissed his prodigal son when he returned (Luke 15:20). Before the feast was spread, before the music and the dance began, the father fell upon his son's neck and kissed him. Our part is to return that kiss. Just as Jesus gives the reconciling kiss on God's behalf, it is our part to kiss Jesus and to prove by that deed that we are *reconciled with God by the death of his Son* (Romans 5:10).

Sinner, until now you have been an enemy of Christ's gospel. You have hated His Sabbaths and neglected His Word. You have despised His commandments and cast His laws behind your back. You have, as much as was in your power, opposed His kingdom. You have loved the wages of sin and the ways of iniquity better than the ways of Christ.

What do you have to say for yourself? Does the Spirit now strive in your heart? Then I urge you to yield to His gracious influence and let your quarrel be at an end. Throw down the weapons of your rebellion, pull out the feathers of pride from your helmet, and cast away the sword of your rebellion. Be His enemy no longer, for rest assured that He desires to be your friend. With arms outstretched and ready to receive you, with eyes full of tears weeping over your stubbornness, and with a heart moved with compassion for you, He speaks through me and says, *Kiss the Son* (Psalm 2:12); be reconciled.

The very message of the gospel is *the ministry of reconciliation* (2 Corinthians 5:18). We speak as God has commanded us. *Now then we are ambassadors for Christ, as though God did exhort you by us; we beseech you in Christ's name, be ye reconciled to God* (2 Corinthians 5:20). Is this a difficult thing we ask of you, that you should be friends with Him who is your best friend? Is this a harsh law, like the commands of Pharaoh to the children of Israel in Egypt, when God asks you to simply shake hands with Him who shed His blood for sinners?

We do not ask you to be the friends of death or hell, but we beg you to dissolve your association with them. We pray that grace may lead you to reject their company forever and be at peace with Him who is incarnate love and infinite mercy. Sinners, why will you resist Him who only desires to save you? Why treat with contempt Him who loves you? Why trample on the blood that bought you and reject the cross, which is the only hope of your salvation?

Mankind is utterly ruined and destroyed. He is lost in a wild waste wilderness. The goatskin bottle of his righteousness is all dried up, and there is not so much as a drop of water in it. The heavens refuse him rain, and the earth can yield him no moisture. Must he perish? He looks above, beneath, around, and he discovers no means of escape. Must he die? Must thirst devour him? Must he fall upon the desert and leave his bones to bleach under the hot sun?

No, for the Scriptures declare that there is a fountain of life. *For with thee is the fountain of life; in thy light shall we see light* (Psalm 36:9). Ordained in eternity past by God in solemn covenant, this fountain, this divine well, takes its spring from the deep foundations of God's decrees. It gushes up from the depth which lies beneath, it comes from that place that the eagle's eye has not seen and the lion's cub has not passed over. The deep foundations of God's government, the depths of

His own essential goodness and of His divine nature –
these are the mysterious springs from which the water
of life gushes forth which will do good to us.

The Son dug this well and bored through massive
rocks which prevented this living water from springing
upward. Using His cross as the grand instrument, He
has pierced through rocks. He has descended to the
lowest depth and has broken open a passage by which
the love and grace of God, the living water that can
save the soul, may well up and overflow to quench the
thirst of dying men and women.

The Son has commanded this fountain to flow freely.
He has removed the stone that covered the mouth of
the fountain, and now having ascended on high, He
stands there to see that the fountain will never stop its
life-giving course, that its floods will never be dry and
its depths will never be exhausted. This sacred fountain,
established according to God's good will and pleasure
in the covenant, opened by Christ when He died upon
the cross, flows this day to give life, health, joy, and
peace to poor sinners who are dead in sin and ruined
by the fall. There is a water of life.

Pause awhile and look at its floods as they come
gushing upward, overflowing on every side and satisfying people's thirst. Let us look with joy. It is called
the water of life, and it richly deserves its name. God's
favor is life, and in His presence there is pleasure for-
evermore. *In thy presence is fullness of joy; in thy right
hand there are pleasures for evermore* (Psalm 16:11). This
water is God's favor, and consequently, it is life. This
water of life is intended to bring God's free grace and

God's love for you, so if you come and drink, you will indeed find this to be life to your soul; for in drinking of God's grace, you inherit God's love, and you are reconciled to God. God stands in a fatherly relation to you. He loves you, and His great infinite heart is filled with compassion toward you.

It is not living water simply because it is love and life, but it also saves from impending death. The sinner knows that he must die because he is unworthy. He has committed sins so tremendous that God must punish him. God would cease to be just if He didn't punish the sins of mankind. When conscious that he has been very guilty, man stands shivering in the presence of his Maker, feeling in his soul that his doom is signed and sealed and that he must certainly be cast away from all hope, life, and joy.

Come, you who are doomed because of your sin. This water can wash away your sins, and when your sins are washed away, then you will live, for the innocent must not be punished. Here is water that can make you whiter than driven snow. Even though your heart is as black as Kedar's smoky tents, here is water that can cleanse you and wash you to the whiteness of perfection and make you as beautiful as the curtains of King Solomon. These waters fully deserve the name of life, since pardon is a condition of life. Unpardoned we die, we perish, we sink into the depths of hell. If pardoned, though, we live, we rise, we ascend to the very heights of heaven. This ever-gushing fountain will give life from the dead to all who take of it, by the pardon of their sins.

"But," one might say, "I have a longing within me that I cannot satisfy. I feel sure that if I am pardoned there will still be something that I need – that nothing I have ever heard of or have ever seen or handled can satisfy. I have within me an aching void that the world can never fill."

"There was a time," says another, "when I was satisfied with the theater, when the amusements and the pleasures of people of the world were very satisfying to me. I have pressed that olive until it no longer yields its generous oil, but it is only the contaminated, thick dregs that I can now obtain. My joys have faded. The beauty of my lush valley has become as a faded flower. I can no longer rejoice in the music of this world."

O soul, I am glad that your cistern has become dry, because until people are dissatisfied with this world, they never look out for the next. Until the god of this world has utterly deceived them, they will not look to Him who is the only living and true God. Listen, you who are wretched and miserable. Here is living water that can quench your thirst! Come and drink, and you will be satisfied, for he who believes in Christ finds enough for him in Christ now, and enough forever.

The believer is not someone who has to pace his room saying, "I find no amusements and no delight." He is not someone whose days are weary and whose nights are long, for he finds in Christ such a spring of joy, such a fountain of consolation, that he is content and happy. Put him in a dungeon and he will find good company. Place him in a barren wilderness, and he would still eat the bread of heaven. Drive him away from friendship, and he will find the *friend that sticks closer than a brother* (Proverbs 18:24). Take away all his shade and shelter, and he will find shadow beneath the Rock of Ages. Destroy the foundation of his earthly hopes, but since the foundation of his God stands sure, his heart will still be firm, trusting in the Lord (Psalm 112:7).

There is such a fulness in Christianity that I can honestly testify that I never knew what happiness was until I knew Christ. I thought I did. I warmed my hands by the fire of sin, but it was a painted fire. When I tasted the Savior's love just once and was washed in Jesus's blood, that was heaven begun below. Oh, if you knew the joys of true Christianity, if you only knew the sweetness of love to Christ, surely you could not stand at a distance. If you could catch just a glimpse of the believer when he is full of joy, you would renounce your wildest fun and your greatest joy to become the lowest child in the family of God. You see that it is the living water. It is the water of life, because it satisfies our thirst and gives us the reality of life that we can never find in anything beneath the sky.

> Stay away from everything that keeps the willing sinner from Christ.

In the name of Almighty God, stay away from everything that keeps the willing sinner from Christ. Away with you, away with you! Christ sprinkles His blood upon the way, and He cries to you, "Vanish, be gone, leave the road clear. Let him come. Do not stand in his path. Make his way straight before him. Level the mountains and fill up the valleys. Make a highway straight through the wilderness for him to come, to drink of this Water of Life freely. Let him come! Oh, that is a precious word of command, because it has all the might of Omnipotence in it! *God said, Let there be light, and there was light* (Genesis 1:3). He says, *Let him that is thirsty come,* and come he will and must. He must be willing to come. *And the Spirit and the bride say, Come. And let him that hears say, Come. And let him that is thirsty come; and whosoever will, let him take of the water of life freely* (Revelation 22:17). Sinner, remember – God says, *Come.* Is there anything in your way? Remember, He adds *Let him come.* He commands everything to move out of your way. Will you come?

Chapter 13

Though One Rose
from the Dead

Human beings are very reluctant to think poorly of themselves, and most are very prone to make excuses for sin. They say, "If we had lived in better times, we would have been better people. If we had been born into this world with better examples, we would have been holier. If we had been placed in better circumstances, we would have been more inclined to do right."

The majority of people, when they seek the cause of their sin, seek it anywhere but in the right place. They will not blame their own nature for it or find fault with their own corrupt heart, but they will lay the blame anywhere else. Some of them find fault with their peculiar position. "If," says one, "I had been born rich instead of being poor, I would not have been dishonest."

"If," says another, "I had been born into the middle class instead of being rich, I would not have been exposed to such temptations of lust and pride as I am now; but my very position is so unfavorable to piety, that I am compelled by my place in society to be anything but what I ought to be."

Others turn around and find fault with the whole of society. They say that the whole structure of society is wrong. They tell us that everything in government, everything that concerns the state, and everything that melts people into societies is all so bad that they cannot be good while things are what they are. They believe they must have a revolution and change everything before they could ever be holy!

Many, on the other hand, throw the blame on their training. If they had not been brought up by their parents in a certain way or if they had not been exposed to certain things in their youth, they would not have been what they are. It is their parents' fault. They lay the sin at their father's or their mother's door.

Or it is their physical constitution. Hear them speak for themselves: "If I had the same demeanor as So-and-so, what a good person I would be! But with my stubborn disposition, it is impossible. It is all very well intentioned to talk to me, but people have different characters, and my personality is such that I couldn't by any means be sincerely pious."

Others go a great deal farther and throw the blame on the ministry. They say, "If the minister had been more passionate in preaching, I would have been a better person. If it had been my privilege to sit under sounder doctrine and hear the Word more faithfully preached, I would have been better." Some lay the blame at the door of professors of Christianity and say,

"If the church were more consistent, if there were no hypocrites and no formalists, then we would change!"

You are putting the saddle on the wrong horse and laying the burden on the wrong back. The blame is in your heart, and nowhere else. If your heart were renewed, you would be better. Until that is done, if society were remodeled to perfection, if ministers were angels and professors of Christianity were seraphs, you wouldn't be any better. Having less excuse, you would be doubly guilty, and you would perish with a more terrible destruction. However, people will always make the excuse that if things were different, they would be different too. If they see the truth, though, they know that the difference must be made in themselves.

> The blame is in your heart, and nowhere else.

If a preacher came from another world to preach to us, we would naturally suppose that he came from heaven. Even the rich man did not ask that he or any of his companions in torment might leave hell to preach (see Luke 16:19-31). Spirits that are lost and given up to unutterable wickedness could not visit this earth, and if they did, they could not preach the truth or lead us on the road to heaven that they had not traveled themselves. The occurrence of a damned spirit upon earth would be a curse, a blight, a withering blast. We have no reason to suppose that such a thing ever did or could occur. The preacher from another world, if such a person could come, would come from heaven. He must be a Lazarus who had lain in Abraham's bosom as a pure, perfect, and holy being.

Imagine for a moment that such a one had descended upon earth. Suppose that we heard that a revered spirit who had been buried for a long time had suddenly burst from his grave clothes, lifted up his coffin lid, and was now preaching the Word of Life. What a rush there would be to hear him preach! What place in this wide world would be large enough to hold the massive congregations? How many thousands of pictures would be published of him, showing him in his grave clothes or as an angel fresh from heaven? Faraway nations would soon hear the news, and every ship and plane would be filled with passengers bringing men and women to hear this wondrous preacher and traveler who had returned from the great unknown. How you would listen, and how solemnly you would gaze at that unearthly spirit! Your ears would pay attention to his every word! His faintest syllable would be recorded and published everywhere throughout the world – the utterances of a man who had been dead and was alive again.

We might want to suppose that if such a thing happened, there would be numberless conversions, thinking that surely the congregations attracted by this would be immensely blessed. Many hardened sinners would be led to repent, and hundreds of those who had been putting off a decision would be made to decide, and much good would be done.

Stop! Even if the first part of the imaginary dream occurred, the second would still not happen. If someone rose from the dead, sinners would not be any more likely to repent through his preaching than through the preaching of any other. God might bless such preaching to salvation if He desired, but in itself there would be no more power in the preaching of the risen dead man or of the glorified spirit than there is of feeble man today. *And he said unto him, If they do not hear Moses and the prophets, neither will they be persuaded, even though one rose from the dead* (Luke 16:31).

If the testimony of one man who had been raised from the dead were of any value for confirming the gospel, would not God have used it before now? It is undoubtedly true that some have risen from the dead. We find accounts in Holy Scripture of some men who by the power of Christ Jesus, or through the instrumentality of prophets, were raised from the dead, but you will note this memorable fact, that not a single one of them spoke one word that is recorded, telling us what they saw while they were dead. Oh, what secrets he could have told us, who laid in his grave four days (see John 11)! Do you not suppose that his sisters questioned him? Do you not think that they asked him what he saw, whether he had stood before the burning throne of God, if he had been judged for the things done in his body, and whether he had entered into rest? They may have asked, but it is certain that he gave no answer. Had he given an answer, we would know it now. Tradition would have cherished the record.

Do you remember when Paul preached a long sermon, even until midnight, and there was a young man in the third-floor window named Eutychus (see Acts 20:7-12)? He fell asleep, fell down, and was taken up dead. Paul came down and prayed, and Eutychus was restored to life. Did Eutychus get up and preach after he had come back from the dead? No. The thought never seems to have struck a single person in the assembly. Paul went on with his sermon, and they sat and listened to him. They did not care one bit about what Eutychus had seen, because Eutychus had nothing more to tell them than Paul had. Of all the ones who by divine might have been brought back from the shades of death, we don't have one secret told or one mystery unraveled by any of them.

Even if someone would rise from the dead and confirm the truth of the gospel, the unbeliever would be no more near believing than now. Here comes Mr. Infidel Critic. He denies the evidences of the Bible that so clearly prove its authenticity that we are required to believe that he is either blasphemous or senseless, and we leave him his choice between the two. He dares to deny the truth of Holy Scripture and insists that all the miracles it contains are untrue and false.

Do you think that one who had risen from the dead could persuade such a man as that to believe? What? When God's whole creation having been ransacked by the hand of science has only testified to the truth of revelation? When the whole history of buried cities and departed nations has only provided evidence that the Bible was true? When every strip of land mentioned in the Bible has been an exposition and a confirmation of the prophecies of Scripture? If people are still unconvinced, do you suppose that one dead man rising from the tomb would convince them?

No. I see the critical blasphemer already armed for his prey. Listen to him: "I am not quite sure that you were ever dead. Sir, you profess to be risen from the dead, but I do not believe you. You say you have been dead and have gone to heaven. My dear man, you must have been in a trance. You must bring proof from the obituaries that you were dead."

The proof is brought that he was dead. "Well, now you must prove that you were buried." It is proved that he was buried, and it is proved that some grave digger in old times took up his dry bones and cast his dust in the air.

"That is very good. Now I want you to prove that you are the identical man who was buried."

"Well I am. I know I am. I tell you as an honest man, I have been to heaven and have come back again."

"Well then," says the unbeliever, "it is not consistent with reason. It is ridiculous to suppose that a man who was dead and buried could ever come to life again. I don't believe you, and I tell you so straight to your face."

That is how people would answer him. Instead of having only the sin of denying many miracles, they would have to add to it the guilt of denying yet another; but they would not even be as much as a tenth of an inch nearer to being convinced. Certainly, if the wonder were done in some far-off land and only reported to the rest of the world, I can imagine that the whole unbelieving world would exclaim, "Simple childish tales and such traditions have been accepted elsewhere, but we are sensible people and do not believe them."

Even if an entire church graveyard would come to life and stand up before the unbeliever who denies the truth of Christianity, I do not believe there would be enough evidence in all the graveyards in the world to convince him. Unbelief would still cry for something more. It is like the horse leech mentioned in Proverbs 30:15. It cries, "Give, give!" Prove a point to an unbeliever, and he wants it proved again. Even if it's as clear as the light of noon to him from the testimony of many witnesses, he still will not believe it. In fact, he does believe it, but he pretends not to, and is an unbeliever in spite of himself. Certainly the dead man's rising would not be worth much to convince such people.

The most numerous class of unbelievers are people who never think at all. There are a great number of people in this land who eat and drink, and do everything else except think. At least they think enough to open their shops in the morning and close them at night. They think enough to know a little about the stock market, or the interest rate, or something like how their merchandise is selling, or the price of bread; but their brains seem to be given to them for nothing at all, except to meditate upon bread and cheese.

To them, following Jesus is a matter of very small concern. They will say that the Bible is very true and that Christianity is alright, but these things do not concern them much. They suppose they are Christians because they were baptized when they were babies. They must be Christians, or at least they suppose they are, but they never stop and ask what real Christianity is. They sometimes go to church, but it does not mean much to them. One minister might contradict another, but they do not know; they dare say they are both right. One minister might be far from another in almost every doctrine, but it does not matter to them.

They pass over Christianity with an unorthodox idea. They say, "God Almighty will not ask us what we believed or if we went to a church that taught what the Bible says." They do not exercise good judgment at all. Thinking is such hard work for them that they never trouble themselves at all about it. If someone were to rise from the dead tomorrow, these people would never even be startled. They would go and see him once, just as they go and see any other curiosity, like the living skeleton or Tom Thumb. They would talk about him a good deal and say, "There's a man risen from the dead!" Some winter evening, they might possibly read one of his sermons, but they would never trouble themselves to consider whether his testimony was true or not.

No. They are so set in their ways that they could never consider any other. If a dead person raised to life were to come to any of their houses, the most they would feel would be that they were somewhat frightened, but as to what the person said, that would never exercise their dull brains or stir their stony senses to even consider truth. Even if one would rise from the dead, the great majority of these people would never be affected.

If Moses and the prophets have failed, no outward means in the world can ever bring you to the footstool of divine grace and make you a Christian. All that can be done now is that God the Spirit must bless the Word to you; otherwise, conscience cannot awaken you, reason cannot awaken you, powerful appeals cannot awaken you, and persuasion cannot bring you to Christ. Nothing will ever do it except God the Holy Spirit.

Chapter 14

The Castle of Self

S trange to say, the majority of those who are saved are the most unlikely people in the world to have been saved, while many of those who perish were once the very people whom we would have expected to see in heaven. There is one who as a child found himself in trouble and in foolishness all the time. His mother often wept over him, and cried and groaned over her son's wanderings. With his fierce spirit that could not be bridled and with his constant rebellions and eruptions of fierce anger, she said, "My son, my son, what will you be like in your later years? Surely, you will smash law and order to pieces and be a disgrace to your father's name."

He grew up. In his youth he was wild and shameless, but wonder of wonders, all of a sudden he became a new man, altogether changed. He was no longer like what he was before, any more than angels are like lost spirits. He sat at his mother's feet and cheered her heart, and the lost, fiery one became gentle, mild, humble as a little child, and obedient to God's commandments.

You say, wonder of wonders! Here, though, is another man. He was a beautiful child and often talked of Jesus. Often, when his mother had him on her knee, he asked her questions about heaven. He was a great example and a wonder of piety in his youth. As he grew up, tears rolled down his cheeks under any sermon. He could scarcely bear to hear of death without a sigh. Sometimes his mother found him alone in prayer.

What is he now? He has become a slave to sin. He has become a corrupt, desperate lowlife. He is deeply entrenched in all types of wickedness, lust, and sin, and has become more corrupt than others could have ever imagined. His own evil spirit, once confined, has now developed itself, and he has learned to play the lion in his manhood, just as he used to play the fox in his youth.

> God has taken the low things of the world and has picked His people out from among the very roughest of men.

This is very often the case. Some abandoned, wicked fellow has had his heart broken and has cried to God for mercy and renounced his vile sin, while some nice church-attending young girl by his side has heard the same sermon, and if there was a tear, she brushed it away. She still continues just as she was, *having no hope, and without God in the world* (Ephesians 2:12). God has taken the low things of the world and has picked His people out from among the very roughest of men, in order that He may prove that it is not natural disposition, but that *saving comes of the LORD* alone (Jonah 2:9).

With sinners, this doctrine is a great battering ram against their pride. I will give you an example. The sinner in his natural condition reminds me of a man who has a strong and nearly impenetrable castle into which he has fled. There is the outer moat, a second moat, and high walls. After that, there is the dungeon and main tower, into which the sinner will withdraw. The first moat that goes around the sinner's trusting place is his good works. "Ah!" he says, "I am as good as my neighbor. I have always paid my debts; I am no sinner. I give to some charities. I'm a good respectable gentleman indeed."

Well, when God comes to work with him, to save him, He sends his army across the first moat. As they go through it, they cry, *Salvation is of the Lord*, and the moat is dried up, for if it is of the Lord, how can it be of good works? But when that is gone, he has a second entrenchment – that of ceremonies.

"Well," he says, "I will not trust in my good works, but I have been baptized, I have been confirmed, and I religiously take the sacrament. That will be my trust."

"Over the moat! Over the moat!" And the soldiers go over again, shouting, *Salvation is of the Lord*. The second moat is dried up, and the trust in ceremonies is gone. Then the soldiers come to the first strong wall. The sinner, looking over it, says, "I can repent. I can believe whenever I like. I will save myself by repenting and believing."

Up come the soldiers of God and His great army

of conviction, and they batter this wall to the ground, crying, *Salvation is of the Lord!* Your faith and your repentance must all be given to you, or you will neither believe nor repent of sin.

The castle is now taken. The man's hopes are all cut off, and he feels that salvation is not of self. The castle of self is overcome, and the great banner upon which is written "Salvation is of the Lord" is displayed upon the battlements.

But is the battle over? Oh, no. The sinner has withdrawn to the tower in the center of the castle, and now he changes his tactics. "I cannot save myself," he says, "therefore, I will despair. There is no salvation for me."

This second part of the castle is as hard to take as the first, for the sinner sits down and says, "I cannot be saved. I must perish." But God commands the soldiers to take this castle, too, shouting, *Salvation is of the Lord.* It is not of man, but it is of God. *He is able also to save to the uttermost,* even though you cannot save yourself (Hebrews 7:25).

This sword, you see, cuts two ways. It cuts pride down, and then it cleaves the skull of despair. If anyone says he can save himself, it cuts his pride in half at once; if someone else says he cannot be saved, it dashes his despair to the earth, for it affirms that he can be saved, seeing that *salvation is of the Lord.*

What is the opposite of this truth? *Salvation is of God*; therefore, damnation is of man. If any of you perish, the blame will not lie at God's door. If you are lost and cast away, you will have to bear all the blame and all the tortures of conscience yourself. You will lie forever in hell and reflect, "I have destroyed myself. I have made a suicide of my soul. I have been my own destroyer, and I can lay no blame on God." Remember, if you are to be saved, you must be saved by God alone, and if you are lost, you have lost yourselves. *Turn ye, turn ye from your evil ways; for why will ye die, O house of Israel?* (Ezekiel 33:11).

Chapter 15

Wavering Between Two Opinions

Most of the people prior to Elijah thought that Jehovah was God, and that Baal was god, too. For this reason, the worship of both was quite consistent. The great majority of people did not reject the God of their fathers wholly, nor did they bow before Baal wholly. As polytheists, believing in many gods, they thought both gods could be worshipped, and each could have a share in their hearts.

"No," said the prophet when he began, "this will not do; these are two different positions. You can never make them one. They are two contradictory things which cannot be combined. Instead of combining the two, which is impossible, you are wavering between the two, which makes a vast difference."

"I will build in my house," said one of them, "an altar for Jehovah here, and an altar for Baal there. I am of one position. I believe them both to be God."

"No, no," said Elijah, "it cannot be so. They are two, and they must be two. These things are not one, but two distinct positions. You cannot unite them."

Many say, "I am worldly, but I am religious, too. I can go worship God on Sunday. I can also go to the races any other time. I go, on the one hand, to the place where I can serve my lusts, and I am met with entertainment in every room of every description. At the same time, I say my prayers most devoutly. Is it not possible to be a good Christian and a man of the world, too? Can I not hold with the hounds as well as run with the hare? May I not love God and serve the devil, too, taking pleasure from each of them, while giving my heart to neither?"

We answer, "No. They are two positions. You cannot do it, because they are distinct and separate."

Mark Antony yoked two lions to his chariot, but there are two lions which no man has ever yoked together: the Lion of the tribe of Judah and the lion of the pit. These can never go together. You can hold two opinions in politics, perhaps, but you will be despised by everybody unless you are of one opinion or the other and act as an independent person. However, you cannot hold two opinions in the matter of your soul and Christianity. If God is God, serve Him and serve Him fully. If this world is god, serve it and do not claim to be a Christian.

If you think the things of the world are the best, serve them; devote yourself to them, grieve your conscience, and run into sin. But remember, if the Lord is your God, you cannot have Baal too. You must have one thing or the other. *No one can serve two masters* (Matthew 6:24). If you serve God, He is your master. If you serve the devil, he will be your master, and you cannot serve two masters.

Be wise and do not think that the two can be mingled together. Many a respectable deacon thinks that he can be covetous and greedy in business and try to take advantage of the poor, and still be a saint. He is a liar to God and to man! He is no saint. He is the very chief of sinners.

Many a very excellent woman is received into church fellowship among the people of God and thinks herself one of the elect, but is found full of wrath and bitterness. She is a slave of mischief and sin, a tattler, a slanderer, and a busybody. She enters into other people's houses and turns everything like comfort out of the minds of those with whom she comes in contact. Still she believes that she is the servant of God and of the devil, too! No, my lady, this will not work. The two can never be served completely. Serve your master, whoever he is. If you do profess to be a Christian, be so completely. If you are not a Christian, do not pretend to be. If you love the world, then love it, but cast off your mask and do not be a hypocrite.

> If you do profess to be a Christian, be so completely.

The double-minded person is the most despicable of all people. He is the follower of Janus, who wears two faces. He can look with one eye upon the (so-called) Christian world with great delight, and donate a little money to the Tract Society, the Bible Society, and the

Missionary Society, but he has another eye over there, with which he looks at the casino, the pub, and other pleasures, which I do not care to mention, but which some may know more of than I wish to know. Such a person is worse than the most corrupt, in the opinion of anyone who knows how to judge. He might not seem worse in his open character, but he really is worse, because he is not honest enough to go through with what he professes.

Tom Loker, in *Uncle Tom*, was pretty near the mark when he shut the mouth of Haley, the slaveholder, who professed religion, with the following common-sense remark: "I can stand most any talk of yours, but your pious talk – that kills me right up. After all, what's the odds between me and you? 'Tain't that you care one bit more or have a bit more feelin' – it's clean, sheer, dog meanness, wanting to cheat the devil and save your own skin; don't I see through it? And your getting religious, as you call it, after all, is a deal too mean for me. Run up a bill with the devil all your life, and then sneak out when pay time comes."

How many do the same every day in London, in England, and everywhere else! They try to serve both masters, but it cannot be. The two things cannot be reconciled. God and greedy gain, Christ and Belial – these never can meet. There can never be an agreement between them, and they can never be brought into unity. Why would you even want to do so? *Two opinions,* said the prophet. He would not allow any of his hearers to profess to worship both. *And Elijah came near unto all the people and said, How long shall ye halt between two opinions? If the LORD is God, follow him; but if Baal, then follow him. And the people did not answer him a word* (1 Kings 18:21).

It was a day to be remembered when the multitudes of Israel were assembled at the foot of Carmel, and the solitary prophet of the Lord came forward to defy the four hundred and fifty priests of the false god. We could look upon that scene with the eye of historical curiosity, and we would find it rich with interest. Instead of doing that, however, we will look at it with the eye of attentive consideration and see if we cannot improve our lives by its teachings.

There are three kinds of people upon that hill of Carmel and along the plain. First, we have the devoted servant of Jehovah, a solitary prophet. On the other hand, we have the decided servants of the evil one – the four hundred and fifty prophets of Baal. However, the great majority of people that day belonged to a third group. They were those who had not fully determined whether to worship Jehovah – the God of their fathers, or Baal – the god of Jezebel.

On the one hand, their ancient traditions led them to fear Jehovah, and on the other hand, their interest in pleasing their leaders and keeping their positions led them to bow before Baal. Therefore, many of them were secret and half-hearted followers of Jehovah, but public worshippers of Baal. All of them at this time were wavering, or halting, between two opinions.

Elijah does not address his sermon to the priests of Baal. He will have something to say to them later, as he will preach them dreadful sermons in deeds of blood.

Nor does Elijah have anything to say to those who are dedicated servants of Jehovah, for they are not there. His discourse is directed specifically to those who are wavering between two positions.

"Now," says the prophet, "if the Lord is God, follow Him. Let your conduct be consistent with what you claim to believe. If you believe the Lord to be God, live it out in your daily life. Be holy, be prayerful, trust in Christ, be faithful, be upright, be loving. Give your whole heart to God and follow Him. If Baal is god, then follow him, but do not pretend to follow the God of Israel."

Let your conduct back up your opinion. If you really think that the foolishness of this world is best, and if you believe that a fashionable life, a life of frivolity and fun, flying from flower to flower while getting honey from none, is the most desirable, then live it out. If you think the life of the pleasure seeker is so very desirable, if you think his end is to be desired, if you think his pleasures are right, then follow them. Go all the way with them. If you believe that to cheat in business is right, put a sign up over your door: *I sell dishonest goods here.*

Do not deceive the public. If you intend to be a real Christian, follow your conviction completely; but if you intend to be worldly, go all the way with the world. Let your conduct follow your opinions, and make your life conform with what you say. Live out your beliefs, whatever they are. But you don't dare to do so, because you are too cowardly to sin honestly and openly before God, as others do. Your conscience will not let you.

How long will you halt between two opinions? You middle-aged men, you said when you were youths, "When we begin our careers, we will follow Jesus. Let us sow our wild oats while we are young, and then we will begin to be diligent servants of the Lord." Now you have come to middle age and are waiting until your new home is built and you will retire; then you think you will serve God. Sirs, you said the same when you began your careers and when your business began to increase. Therefore, I demand of you, "How long will you halt between two opinions?" How much time do you want?

How long will you halt between two opinions?

Young man, you said in your early childhood, when your mother's prayer followed you, "I will seek God when I become a man." You have passed that day. You are a man, and more than that, and you are still wavering. *How long shall ye halt between two opinions?*

Many of you have attended church for years. You have been under the conviction of the Spirit of God many times, but you have wiped the tears from your eyes and said, "I will seek God and turn to Him with full purpose of heart." Now, you are just where you were then. How many more sermons do you need? How many more Sundays must be wasted? How many warnings, how many sicknesses, how many times must the bell toll to warn you that you must die? How many graves must be dug for your family before an impression will be made upon you? How many plagues and pestilences must ravage this city before you will turn to God in truth? *How long shall ye halt between two opinions?* I pray that you would answer this question and not allow the sands of life to drop, drop, drop from the glass saying, "When the next one goes I will repent," yet that next one finds you unrepentant still.

You say, "When the glass reaches a certain point, I will turn to God." No. It is pointless to talk this way, because you may find your glass empty before you thought it had begun to run low. You may find yourself in eternity when you thought you would get around to repenting and turning to God.

The prophet cries, *If the LORD is God, follow him; but if Baal, then follow him* (1 Kings 18:21). In so doing, he states the basis of his practical claim. Let your conduct be consistent with your beliefs.

Another objection is raised by the crowd. "Prophet," someone says, "you come to demand practical proof of our affection. You say, 'Follow God.' Now, if I believe God to be God, and that is my opinion, I still do not see what right He has to lay claim to my beliefs."

Now, pay attention to how the prophet puts it. He says, *If the LORD is God, follow him.* The reason I claim that you should put action behind your opinion concerning God is that God is God! God has a claim upon you, as creatures, for your devoted obedience.

Someone replies, "What profit would I have if I served God completely? Would I be happier? Would I do better in this world? Would I have more peace of mind?"

No. Those are secondary considerations. The only thing for you to consider is, *If the LORD is God, follow him.* Not if it is more advantageous to you, but

If the LORD is God, follow him. A worldly religious person might plead for Christianity on the grounds that Christianity might be the best for this world and best for the world to come. Not so with the prophet. He says, "I do not base it on that reasoning. Instead, I insist that it is your bound duty that if you believe in God you must serve Him and obey Him simply because He is God. I do not tell you it is for your advantage; it may be, and I believe it is, but I put that aside from the question. I demand of you that you follow God if you believe Him to be God. If you do not think He is God, if you really think that the devil is god, then follow him. His pretended godhead will be your plea, and you will be consistent; but if God is God, if He made you, I demand that you serve Him. If it is He who puts breath into your nostrils, I demand that you obey Him. If God is really worthy of worship, and you really think so, I demand that you either follow Him, or else deny that He is God at all."

How long shall ye halt between two opinions? I will tell them. You will halt between two opinions, all of you who are undecided, until God answers by fire. Fire was not what these poor people who were assembled there wanted. Elijah proclaimed that *the God that answers by fire is God* (1 Kings 18:24).

I imagine that I hear some of them saying, "No, the God who answers by water, let Him be God. We need rain badly enough."

"No," said Elijah, "if rain would come, you would say that it was the common course of nature, and that would not lead you to decide." I tell you, nothing that comes from God and nothing that God sends into your life will cause you who are undecided to decide. God may surround you with His care, influences, and intervention. He may surround you with frequent warnings from the deathbed of your fellow men, but these things will never cause you to make a decision.

It is not the God of rain, but the God of fire who will do it. There are two ways in which you who are undecided will be decided in the future. You who have decided to follow God will need no decision. You who have decided to follow Satan will need no decision; you are on Satan's side and must dwell forever in eternal burning.

However, you who are undecided need something to help you decide. You will have one of two things: you will either have the fire of God's Spirit to lead you to decide, or your decision will be made by the fire of eternal judgment.

> *Answer me, O LORD, answer me, that this people may know that thou art the LORD God and that thou shalt convert their heart back again to thee.* (1 Kings 18:37)

Charles H. Spurgeon – A Brief Biography

Charles Haddon Spurgeon was born on June 19, 1834, in Kelvedon, Essex, England. He was one of seventeen children in his family (nine of whom died in infancy). His father and grandfather were Nonconformist ministers in England. Due to economic difficulties, eighteen-month-old Charles was sent to live with his grandfather, who helped teach Charles the ways of God. Later in life, Charles remembered looking at the pictures in *Pilgrim's Progress* and in *Foxe's Book of Martyrs* as a young boy.

Charles did not have much of a formal education and never went to college. He read much throughout his life though, especially books by Puritan authors.

Even with godly parents and grandparents, young Charles resisted giving in to God. It was not until he was fifteen years old that he was born again. He was on his way to his usual church, but when a heavy snowstorm prevented him from getting there, he turned in at a little Primitive Methodist chapel. Though there were only about fifteen people in attendance, the preacher spoke from Isaiah 45:22: *Look unto me, and be ye saved, all the ends of the earth.* Charles Spurgeon's eyes were opened and the Lord converted his soul.

He began attending a Baptist church and teaching Sunday school. He soon preached his first sermon, and then when he was sixteen years old, he became the pastor of a small Baptist church in Cambridge. The church soon grew to over four hundred people, and Charles Spurgeon, at the age of nineteen, moved on to become the pastor of the New Park Street Church in London. The church grew from a few hundred attenders to a few thousand. They built an addition to the church, but still needed more room to accommodate the congregation. The Metropolitan Tabernacle was built in London in 1861, seating more than 5,000 people. Pastor Spurgeon preached the simple message of the cross, and thereby attracted many people who wanted to hear God's Word preached in the power of the Holy Spirit.

On January 9, 1856, Charles married Susannah Thompson. They had twin boys, Charles and Thomas. Charles and Susannah loved each other deeply, even amidst the difficulties and troubles that they faced in life, including health problems. They helped each other spiritually, and often together read the writings of

Jonathan Edwards, Richard Baxter, and other Puritan writers.

Charles Spurgeon was a friend of all Christians, but he stood firmly on the Scriptures, and it didn't please all who heard him. Spurgeon believed in and preached on the sovereignty of God, heaven and hell, repentance, revival, holiness, salvation through Jesus Christ alone, and the infallibility and necessity of the Word of God. He spoke against worldliness and hypocrisy among Christians, and against Roman Catholicism, ritualism, and modernism.

One of the biggest controversies in his life was known as the "Down-Grade Controversy." Charles Spurgeon believed that some pastors of his time were "down-grading" the faith by compromising with the world or the new ideas of the age. He said that some pastors were denying the inspiration of the Bible, salvation by faith alone, and the truth of the Bible in other areas, such as creation. Many pastors who believed what Spurgeon condemned were not happy about this, and Spurgeon eventually resigned from the Baptist Union.

Despite some difficulties, Spurgeon became known as the "Prince of Preachers." He opposed slavery, started a pastors' college, opened an orphanage, led in helping feed and clothe the poor, had a book fund for pastors who could not afford books, and more.

Charles Spurgeon remains one of the most published preachers in history. His sermons were printed each week (even in the newspapers), and then the sermons for the year were re-issued as a book at the end of the year. The first six volumes, from 1855-1860, are known as *The Park Street Pulpit*, while the next fifty-seven volumes, from 1861-1917 (his sermons continued to be published long after his death), are known as *The Metropolitan Tabernacle Pulpit*. He also oversaw a monthly magazine-type publication called *The Sword and the Trowel*, and Spurgeon wrote many books, including *Lectures to My Students*, *All of Grace*, *Around the Wicket Gate*, *Advice for Seekers*, *John Ploughman's Talks*, *The Soul Winner*, *Words of Counsel for Christian Workers*, *Cheque Book of the Bank of Faith*, *Morning and Evening*, his autobiography, and more, including some commentaries, such as his twenty-year study on the Psalms – *The Treasury of David*.

Charles Spurgeon often preached ten times a week, preaching to an estimated ten million people during his lifetime. He usually preached from only one page of notes, and often from just an outline. He read about six books each week. During his lifetime, he had read *The Pilgrim's Progress* through more than one hundred times. When he died, his personal library consisted of more than 12,000 books. However, the Bible always remained the most important book to him.

Spurgeon was able to do what he did in the power of God's Holy Spirit because he followed his own advice – he met with God every morning before meeting with others, and he continued in communion with God throughout the day.

Charles Spurgeon suffered from gout, rheumatism, and some depression, among other health problems. He often went to Menton, France, to recuperate and rest. He preached his final sermon at the Metropolitan

Tabernacle on June 7, 1891, and died in France on January 31, 1892, at the age of fifty-seven. He was buried in Norwood Cemetery in London.

Charles Haddon Spurgeon lived a life devoted to God. His sermons and writings continue to influence Christians all over the world.

Similar Titles

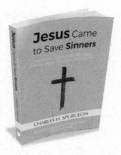

Jesus Came to Save Sinners
by Charles H. Spurgeon

This is a heart-level conversation with you, the reader. Every excuse, reason, and roadblock for not coming to Christ is examined and duly dealt with. If you think you may be too bad, or if perhaps you really are bad and you sin either openly or behind closed doors, you will discover that life in Christ is for you too. You can reject the message of salvation by faith, or you can choose to live a life of sin after professing faith in Christ, but you cannot change the truth as it is, either for yourself or for others. As such, it behooves you and your family to embrace truth, claim it for your own, and be genuinely set free for now and eternity. Come and embrace this free gift of God, and live a victorious life for Him.

Available where books are sold

Faithful to Christ, Charles H. Spurgeon

If there is a true faith, there must be a declaration of it. If you are a candle, and God has lit you, then let your light so shine before men that they may see your good works and glorify your Father who is in the heavens (Matthew 5:16). Soldiers of Christ must, like soldiers of our nation, wear their uniforms; and if they are ashamed of their uniforms, they ought to be drummed out of the army.

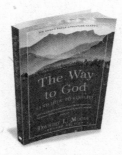

The Way to God, Dwight L. Moody

There is life in Christ. Rich, joyous, wonderful life. It is true that the Lord disciplines those whom He loves and that we are often tempted by the world and our enemy, the devil. But if we know how to go beyond that temptation to cling to the cross of Jesus Christ and keep our eyes on our Lord, our reward both here on earth and in heaven will be 100 times better than what this world has to offer.

This book is thorough. It brings to life the love of God, examines the state of the unsaved individual's soul, and analyzes what took place on the cross for our sins. *The Way to God* takes an honest look at our need to repent and follow Jesus, and gives hope for unending, joyous eternity in heaven.

Available where books are sold

The Overcoming Life, by Dwight L. Moody

Are you an overcomer? Or, are you plagued by little sins that easily beset you? Even worse, are you failing in your Christian walk, but refuse to admit and address it? No Christian can afford to dismiss the call to be an overcomer. The earthly cost is minor; the eternal reward is beyond measure.

Available where books are sold